The Australians

The Australians

INSIDERS & OUTSIDERS ON
THE NATIONAL CHARACTER
SINCE 1770

John HIRST

Black Inc.

Published by Black Inc.,
an imprint of Schwartz Publishing Pty Ltd
Level 5, 289 Flinders Lane
Melbourne Victoria 3000 Australia
email: enquiries@blackincbooks.com
http://www.blackincbooks.com

Document collection © National Australia Day Council, 2007
Section introductions © John Hirst, 2007

The National Australia Day Council is generously supported by the Australian Government through the Department of Prime Minister and Cabinet. The document collection contained in this publication was supported by the Australian Government through the Quality Outcomes Programme administered by the Department of Education, Science and Training.

ALL RIGHTS RESERVED.
No part of this publication may be reproduced, stored in a retrieval system, or transmitted in any form by any means electronic, mechanical, photocopying, recording or otherwise without the prior consent of the publishers.

Every effort has been made to contact the copyright holders of material in this book. However, where an omission has occurred, the publisher will gladly include acknowledgement in any future edition.

The National Library of Australia Cataloguing-in-Publication entry:

> The Australians : insiders and outsiders on the national
> character since 1770.

> 1st ed.
> Includes index.
> ISBN 9781863954082 (pbk.).

> 1. National characteristics, Australian. 2. Australia -
> Quotations, maxims, etc. I. Hirst, J. B. (John Bradley),
> 1942- .

> 994

Book design: Thomas Deverall
Index: Penny Mansley

Printed in Australia by Griffin Press

Contents

Foreword

The Australian Constitution on which our federation is founded begins with the simple words 'Whereas the people ... have agreed to unite'. Nothing could more elegantly capture the idea that the Australian people make the Australian nation.

Every year on Australia Day we celebrate this fact. But the people we are now are different from those that forged those words over a hundred years ago. Or are we? Just who are the Australians? In 2006 the National Australia Day Council commissioned Dr John Hirst, one of our most eminent historians, to explore the question, to examine the nature and the roots of the national character so we might better understand the people we have become. This book is the fruit of his labour.

It offers a diverse range of voices from inside and outside Australia, voices from the past and present that demonstrate how our history remains with us in profound and often unexpected ways. The themes around which the discussion is structured reflect key aspects of our shared collective history as well as the varieties of our experience as Australians. Together they highlight the paradox of a particular identity that is constantly changing.

Dr Hirst has drawn together a fascinating chorus of voices dating from 1770, ranging from the first insightful observations of the Australians from one of the first outsiders, Captain James Cook, to powerful commentary from one of the newest insider Australians in 2006. I am confident these voices will both confirm much of what we believe to be true about us and also challenge many of our ideas about how we became who we are. There may be no simple answer to the question of 'Who are the Australians?'

but Dr Hirst's collection will certainly stimulate considerable discussion of what makes the Australian identity unique.

In understanding our history each of us can make a contribution to build Australia and our national character in the years ahead. Each Australia Day we invite all Australians to acknowledge the past, rejoice in our achievements and look confidently to the future. We look to the past to learn from our successes and our mistakes. While we have inherited a history that powerfully shapes us all, tomorrow's history is ours for the making.

Warren Pearson
National Director
National Australia Day Council

Introduction

This book collects what outsiders have said about Australians and Australian characteristics and what Australians have said about themselves. In some quarters this will be regarded as an unfashionable book because it believes that there is such a thing as an Australian national character.

In 2002 many Australians were killed and injured in the terrorist attack in Bali. At the local hospital there was a shortage of everything the doctors needed, including pain-killers. Graeme Southwick, the Australian doctor who took charge of the 'Australian' ward, asked patients to assess their own pain level. Time and again the patients said they were alright; they told him to give the drugs to the person next to them who was suffering more.

This account awoke a memory in me. I turned to Charles Bean's *Official History* of the Gallipoli campaign to check it. The first wounded taken off the peninsula endured terrible conditions: the preparations had been woeful. But the injured remained cheerful and Bean reports: 'Yet the men never showed better than in these difficulties. The lightly hurt were full of thought for the severely wounded.'

Another Australian doctor in Bali praised the volunteers in the hospital. David Marsh said, 'I think it is what Aussies do. There were well over a hundred there, all Aussies, fanning patients because there was no air-conditioning, standing all day holding up drips because there were no drip stands.'

That brought to mind the makeshift hospitals of 'Weary' Dunlop on the Burma railway. The Australian captives of the Japanese acted differently from the English, the Dutch and the Americans. Gavan Daws in his book *Prisoners of the Japanese* concluded, 'The Australians kept trying to construct little male-bonded welfare states.'

Of the rescue effort at the Bali nightclubs, Neil Williams of the Forbes Rugby Club reported, 'It was fantastic. Good old Aussie spirit. We had fellas manning the fire engines. We had fellas running in pulling people out dead and alive. Everyone stepped right up. It was tremendous.'

At their baptism into the new era of terrorism the qualities that Australians valued were stoicism, making no fuss, pitching in, making do, helping each other. These characteristics were identified and valued as Australian a long time ago, when we were British and our national symbol was a bushman. There has been a long campaign claiming that in a changed world and in a changed Australia, the values and symbols of old Australia are exclusive, oppressive and irrelevant. The campaign does not appear to have succeeded.

There is an absurdity in telling a people to drop their old values and symbols, for these are the things that have made them a people. And yet a people need to change. Those who want change do well to let it flow out of tradition. Otherwise, in the words of Bernhard Philberth, 'a perverted traditionalism and a misguided progressivism propel each other to a deadly excess'.

We have had examples of both tendencies in Australia in recent years. This book is designed to do good service to the nation by tracing both tradition and change in the Australian character. There are old voices and new. There is celebration and criticism.

Outsiders and insiders have had different perspectives on Australia, and Australians have had to deal one way or another with what outsiders – particularly the British – have said about them. There is also a difference between what Australians think of themselves and what they are really like. Australians, like other peoples, tend to think they are highly distinctive, but the characteristics they value may be an extension or an exaggeration of what they brought from the mother country. In some respects they may be more like the peoples of other new lands settled by the British than they are willing to acknowledge. I have been aware of these complexities as I have chosen the extracts; in fact I have chosen them in order that the complexities might be highlighted. I have not of course resolved the complexities, but there is plenty for the reader to ponder.

Those who have attacked the old Australian character and the very notion of a national character argue that a diverse nation has no need to discover or define or celebrate a distinctive character; it should be committed solely to the civic values of democracy, the rule of law and toleration – or better, the welcoming of difference – the values that a liberal nation anywhere needs to cultivate. There may come a time when these are enough, though it is hard to imagine a nation so defined being one to love or die for. Will anyone lay down their life for diversity? For the moment anyway we cannot manage without a sense of what unites us as Australians.

We can check where we stand at present by looking at the government's efforts to protect Muslims in Australia after the September 11 attacks. Prime Minister John Howard, following President George W. Bush's example, visited a mosque. There Muslim spokesmen identified themselves strongly as Australian and the Prime Minister extended to them the 'hand of Australian mateship' and told them they were 'a treasured part of the Australian community'. He urged Australians not to attack Australian Muslims because of the destruction of the twin towers. That is, if Muslims were to be protected they had to be identified as a part of the Australian community. From which I conclude that the civic values are not enough, that if rights are to be protected there must be a community to which people are warmly attached so that they will care about each other's rights. We have to be Australians and go on pondering what that means.

John Hirst

I

Who Are the Australians?

The first people to be called Australians were the Aborigines. The explorer Matthew Flinders, who sailed around the continent in 1802–03 and gave it its name, noticed differences between tribes but used 'Australians' for them all. At this stage the British convict settlement at Sydney was a tiny speck and no-one there thought of themselves as Australian. Soon the Aborigines lost that title and did not regain it until 150 years later. Who had the best right to the title was an ongoing matter of dispute.

THE NATIVES OF THE COUNTRY

When Australians were ashamed of their convict past, they traced the origins of their country not from the settlement at Sydney on 26 January 1788, but from the voyage of Captain Cook along the east coast in 1770. When Aborigines were taught that Australian history began with Cook, they decided that Cook must be an evil character and he appears as such in Aboriginal myths. Actually Cook, as a man of the Enlightenment, took a favourable view of Aborigines and their society. Nevertheless, he did claim the territory on the east coast for the king.

The Natives of this Country are of a middle Stature straight bodied and slender-limb'd, their skins the Colour of Wood soot or of a dark chocolate their hair mostly black, some lank and others curled, they all wear it crop'd short, their Beards which are generally black they likewise crop short or singe off. Their features are far from being disagreeable and their voices are soft and tunable. They go quite naked both men and women without any manner of Cloathing whatever, even the women do not so much as cover their privates. Altho none of us were ever very near any of their women, one Gentleman excepted, yet we are all as well satisfied of this as if we had lived among them. Notwithstanding we had several interviews with the men while we lay in Endeavour River, yet whether through Jealousy or disrigard they never brought any of their Women along with them to the Ship but always left them on the opposite side of the River where we had frequent opportunities viewing them through our glasses. They wear as ornaments Necklaces made of shells, Bracelets, or hoops about their arms, made mostly of hair, twisted and made like a cord hoop, these they wear tight about the uper parts of their arms and some have girdles made in the same manner. The men wear a bone about 3 or 4 Inches long and a fingers thick, run through the Bridge of the nose which the Seamen call'd a spritsail yard, they likewise have holes in their ears for Earrings but we never saw them Wear any.

They seem to have no fix'd habitation but move about from place to place like wild Beasts in search of food, and I believe depend wholy upon the success of the present day for their subsistance. They have Wooden fish gigs with 2, 3 or 4 prongs each very ingeniously made with which they strike fish; we have also seen them strike both fish and birds with their darts. With these they likewise kill other Animals: they have also wooden Harpoons for striking Turtle, but of these I believe they got but few, except at the Season they come a Shore to lay. In short these people live wholy by fishing and hunting, but mostly by the former for we never saw one Inch of Cultivated land in the Whole Country, they know however the use of Taara and sometimes eat them. We do not know that they eat any thing raw but roast or broil all they eat on slow small fires.

From what I have said of the Natives of New-Holland they may appear to some to be the most wretched people upon the earth: but in reality they are far more happier than we Europeans; being wholy unacquainted not only with the superfluous but the necessary Conveniences so much sought after in Europe, they are happy in not knowing the use of them. They live in a Tranquillity which is not disturbed by the Inequality of Condition: The Earth and sea of their own accord furnishes them with all things necessary for life; they covet not Magnificent Houses, Household-stuff &c they live in a warm and fine Climate and enjoy a very wholsome Air: so that they have very little need of Clothing and this they seem to be fully sensible of for many to whome we gave Cloth &c to, left it carelessly upon the Sea beach and in the woods as a thing they had no manner of use for. In short they seem'd to set no value upon anything we gave them nor would they ever part with any thing of their own for any one article we could offer them this in my opinion argues that they think themselves provided with all the necessarys of Life and that they have no superfluities …

SUNBURNT AUSTRALIANS ARE YOUR BRETHREN

As British settlers advanced into Aboriginal lands, they commonly came to regard Aborigines as a low form of life, who could be killed or ignored. A few committed Christians did defend the Aborigines. Robert Lyon, a pioneer settler in Western Australia, believed in the humanity of the Aborigines and that they should become Christians. He persuaded the authorities to allow him to accompany Yagan, the resistance fighter, when he was sent to Carnac Island. He used the term 'Australian' for the Aborigines – and also 'savage', believing with other Christians that the Aborigines must have declined into their present position when they split off from the original human population described in the Bible. Hence the odd title of his book: An Appeal to The World on behalf of the younger branch of the Family of Shem (1839).

Time would fail me to enumerate the many instances of disinterested benevolence shown by the Aborigines to the invaders of their country. They repeatedly recovered strayed stock and brought them to the owners, carrying in their arms the kids and the lambs which they found, while they themselves were wandering through the forest in search of food and famishing with hunger. They treated the lost wanderer with the kindest hospitality, dividing their humble repast with him, allowing him to rest for the night in their camp, and conducting him on his way in the morning. They held the house and the property of the lonely settler sacred, aiding him in his toils when present, and sharing their food with his children when absent. They rescued the fainting soldier and the emaciated explorer from the mazes of the forest; and, not only having saved them from the horrors of famine, but restored them to their families, their friends, and the settlement.

Away with dissimilation. If ye pretend to doubt the sunburnt skin of the Australians, apply the lance to their veins. Even this is needless. Ye have already gone to the fountain head and thrust the pointed steel into their hearts. Examine the crimson fluid, as it pours out – there can be no mistake here – and say, Is it not blood of your own? Yes. The bleeding victims of your avarice are your brethren! To slander an innocent race, in order to justify their extermination, is as cruel as it is cowardly and base. Glory in your apparent security; only flatter not yourselves that vengeance will allow the guilty to escape both in this world and the next. Even in life's short span, ye will have some cause to repent. Ye may disregard the sleeping tribunals of your country; but ye shall not escape the infamy which your deeds justly merit.

How hard is the fate of this people! They may stand to be slaughtered; but they must not throw a spear in their own defence, or attempt to bring their enemies to a sense of justice by the only means in their power, – that of returning like for like. If they do – if they are to be guilty of an act which in other nations would be eulogized as the noblest of a patriot's deeds – they are outlawed; a reward is set upon their heads; and they are ordered to be shot, as if they were so many mad dogs! Thus, in the most barbarous manner, ye practice what in them ye condemn, the law of retaliation.

THE NEW NATIVES

In the 1810s the first generation of British people born in New South Wales came of age. They were called the native-born and they took the name Australian; the slang term for them was 'currency', a reference to the local money supply in contrast to sterling or British money. The badge of a currency lad was the cabbage-tree hat, woven from the fronds of a local palm tree.

In 1823 John Bigge, a royal commissioner sent from Britain, described the native-born in his official report.

The class of inhabitants that have been born in the colony affords a remarkable exception to the moral and physical character of their parents: they are generally tall in person, and slender in their limbs, of fair complexion, and small features. They are capable of undergoing more fatigue, and are less exhausted by labour than native Europeans; they are active in their habits, but remarkably awkward in their movements. In their tempers they are quick and irascible, but not vindictive; and I only repeat the testimony of persons who have had many opportunities of observing them, that they neither inherit the vices nor the feelings of their parents.

Many of the native youths have evinced a strong disposition for a sea-faring life, and are excellent sailors; and no doubt can be entertained that that class of the population will afford abundant and excellent materials for the supply of any department in the commercial or naval service.

*

The Currency Lass, *a musical drama written by a convict, was first performed in Sydney in 1844. The plot turns on the hero's English uncle thinking that his nephew is to marry an Aborigine because the fiancée is described as a 'native'. This is one of its songs, 'The Boy in the Cabbage-Tree Hat'.*

Talk not to me of your Frenchmen or Dons
 Or the graces they claim to inherit.
They're asses compared to Australia's sons,
 The lads for fun, frolic and spirit!
There, grimace and palaver in plenty you'll find,
 Where foppery comes to them pat, sir;
But the ladies I'll ask if not more to their mind
 Is the boy in the cabbage-tree hat, sir.

His heart ever true to his friend and his lass,
 To honour the fair his first duty,
The Currency Lad never flinches his glass
 While he pours the libation to beauty.
Let others then seek by each exquisite art
 To win your applause and all that, sir.
They may make the attempt but they ne'er can compare
 With the boy in the cabbage-tree hat, sir!

NATIVE-BORN ARE TRUE AUSTRALIANS

The gold rushes of the 1850s brought a mass of new settlers and so post-poned for a generation the time when the native-born would be in the majority. In the 1870s and 1880s in Victoria the children of the gold-rush generation came of age. Many of the more sober and respectable young men formed the Australian Natives Association, which defended the reputation of the native-born against the criticisms of their British-born parents and advocated the formation of an Australian nation. It was a standing joke in the Association that they were not Aborigines as was commonly assumed, but the Association did agitate to protect and defend the Aborigines.

George Meudell was one of the most assertive of the 'natives' and the author of 'Australia for the Australians' (1882).

Our present Parliament, no doubt, well represents the successes and failures of our imported society, with its continual struggle to have and to hold; but it is devoid of patriotism, and I maintain that no parliament in which the patriotic element is wanting can have the real and substantial good of the country at heart. Every colonial Britisher considers himself an exile from his fatherland, as he is only here to make money, and never relinquishes the fond idea that 'there is no place like home'.

Every Australian has the feeling, not shared by 'foreigners', that every class interest is limited by, and subordinate to, the interest of the aggregate of the community. This subordination of self and class interest to the interest of all, with the emotional glow which follows and recompenses every act of self-surrender, is the simplest and purest form of patriotism. Knowing, therefore, that the interest of the few is the robbery of the many, the Australian will sternly repress log-rolling and swindling, and will only vote for the man who will represent general and not individual and clique interests. He will be influenced only by a public-spirited desire for the advancement of his native land, and not for the advancement of any particular statesman or party.

*

One of the criticisms that the older generation made of the native-born was that they were too interested in sport and outdoor activities. The Australian Natives Association tried to counter this image by running lectures and debates and devoting themselves to self-improvement. The novelist Rolf Boldrewood sold thousands of copies of Robbery under Arms (1880) with a hero that reinforced the stereotype. These are its opening words.

My name's Dick Marston, Sydney-side native. I'm twenty-nine years old, six feet in my stocking soles, and thirteen stone weight. Pretty strong and active with it, so they say. I don't want to blow – not here any road – but it takes a good man to put me on my back, or stand up to me with the gloves, or the naked mauleys. I can ride anything – anything that was ever lapped in horsehide – swim like a musk-duck, and track like a Myall blackfellow. Most things that a man can do I'm up to, and that's all about it. As I lift myself now I can feel the muscle swell on my arm like a cricket ball, in spite of the – well, in spite of everything.

AUSTRALIANS ARE WHITE MEN

The Sydney Bulletin, published from 1880, was the first national newspaper. It was radical, republican and a fierce advocate of the White Australia policy, which the colonies adopted in 1888 when they passed uniform legislation against Chinese migrants and which the new Commonwealth enshrined in 1901. The Bulletin claimed with some justice that Britain did not want Australia to adopt a White Australia policy.

By the term Australian we mean not those who have merely been born in Australia. All white men who come to these shores – with a clean record – and who leave behind them the memory of class-distinctions and the religious differences of the old world; all men who place the happiness, the prosperity, the advancement of their adopted country before the interests of Imperialism, are Australian. In this regard all men who leave the tyrant-ridden lands of Europe for freedom of speech and right of personal liberty are Australians before they set foot on the ship which brings them hither. Those who fly from an odious military conscription; those who leave their fatherland because they cannot swallow the worm-eaten lie of the divine right of kings to murder peasants, are Australians by instinct – Australian and republican are synonymous. No nigger, no Chinaman, no lascar, no kanaka, no purveyor of cheap coloured labour, is an Australian.

OLD AUSTRALIANS

Aborigines were not thought of as part of the new nation. It was around 1900 that they lost their civil rights so that they could not move or marry without official permission and their children were liable to be taken from them. Aboriginal protests began in the 1920s, and on Australia Day, 26 January 1938, the 150th anniversary of European settlement, Aborigines held a protest meeting in Sydney and issued a pamphlet, Aborigines Claim Citizen Rights, written by J.T. Patten and W. Ferguson, the president and secretary of the Aborigines Progressive Association.

The 26th of January, 1938, is not a day of rejoicing for Australia's Aborigines; it is a day of mourning. This festival of 150 years' so-called 'progress' in Australia commemorates also 150 years of misery and degradation imposed upon the original native inhabitants by the white invaders of this country. We, representing the Aborigines, now ask you, the reader of this appeal, to pause in the midst of your sesqui-centenary rejoicings and ask yourself honestly whether your 'conscience' is clear in regard to the treatment of the Australian blacks by the Australian whites during the period of 150 years' history which you celebrate?

The Old Australians

You are the New Australians, but we are the Old Australians. We have in our arteries the blood of the Original Australians, who have lived in this land for many thousands of years. You came here only recently, and you took our land away from us by force. You have almost exterminated our people, but there are enough of us remaining to expose the humbug of your claim, as white Australians, to be a civilised, progressive, kindly and humane nation. By your cruelty and callousness towards the Aborigines you stand condemned in the eyes of the civilised world.

Plain Speaking

These are hard words, but we ask you to face the truth of our accusations. If you would openly admit that the purpose of your Aborigines Legislation has been, and now is, to exterminate the Aborigines completely so that not a trace of them or of their descendants remains, we could describe you as brutal, but honest. But you dare not admit openly that your hope and wish is for our death! You hypocritically claim that you are trying to 'protect' us; but your modern policy of 'protection' (so-called) is killing us off just as surely as the pioneer policy of giving us poisoned damper and shooting us down like dingoes!

We do not ask for your charity; we do not ask you to study us as scientific freaks. Above all, we do not ask for your 'protection.' No, thanks! We have had 150 years of that! We ask only for justice, decency and fair play. Is this too much to ask? Surely your minds and hearts are not so callous that you will refuse to reconsider your policy of degrading and humiliating and exterminating Old Australia's Aborigines?

NEW AUSTRALIANS

The migrants to Australia came overwhelmingly from England, Scotland and Ireland and here they and their children became British Australians. After World War II the Labor government decided to boost population with a large-scale migration program. In 1945 Arthur Calwell, the minister for immigration, indicated his willingness to look outside Britain for migrants. He urged Australians to call the new non-British migrants New Australians rather than 'wogs' or 'dagos'. But Calwell remained a firm believer in the White Australia policy.

Apart from schemes of organized and assisted British migration, the door to Australia is always open within the limits of our existing legislation to people from the various dominions, the United States of America, and from European continental countries who are sound in health and who will not become a charge on the community, to come here and make their homes. The Australian people must help newcomers to become assimilated. We have been too prone in the past to ostracize those of alien birth and then blame them for segregating themselves and forming foreign communities. It is we, not they, who are generally responsible for this condition of affairs. Fortunately, we have only three areas in Australia where non-British migrants have tended to congregate in considerable numbers. One of these is in Shepparton, Victoria, the second is the Leeton-Griffith irrigation area of New South Wales, and the third is on the northern cane-fields of Queensland. That these people can be absorbed into our community life in the course of one generation is proved by the fact that the Australian-born children of most foreign-born parents have played their part in the fighting services in the defence of Australia in this war and regard themselves as Australian, having equal citizen rights, and bearing equal national responsibilities with every other Australian.

In the United States of America, residence, and not nationality, determines liability for service in the armed forces. Because of United States law, many draftees who were born in enemy countries were sent to fight for the defence of this country in the South-West Pacific Area. In our terminology, they would have been regarded as 'enemy aliens', but by their residence in the United States of America they earned the right to be treated on the same basis as loyal American citizens, and we have to thank them for the part they played in association with our own armed forces and other members of Allied units in saving this country from invasion. It may be well for Australia closely to examine this American attitude, and decide whether this may not be the proper way to treat and assimilate the newcomer.

Unfortunately, campaigns are fostered in this country from time to time on racial and religious grounds by persons who have ulterior motives to serve. The activities of such people cannot be too strongly condemned. They are anti-Australian and anti-Christian, and make not for national unity and national well-being but for the creation of discord and bitterness that is harmful to Australians at home and abroad.

FIRST AUSTRALIANS

Anthropologists played an important role in changing Australian attitudes to Aborigines in the years after World War II. In 1952 the husband and wife team Ronald and Catherine Berndt published a little book The

First Australians, which was one of the first uses of this term for the Aborigines. The book was dedicated to their teacher Professor A.P. Elkin, who in 1938 had written The Australian Aborigines: How to Understand Them. *This is from the introduction to the Berndts' book.*

Let us try to understand and appreciate these First Australians – people who were so admirably adjusted to the environment with which we now, at times, find ourselves in conflict: whose cultures were, and in some places still are, vivid living realities, splashed with brilliant colouring, virile, meaningful: people possessed of a religious zeal and a faith in life, a faith in the essential goodness and significance of their own way – the Aboriginal Way. But this Way was so patterned that its possessors found it hard to combat the alien invader; and it was based on premises contrary to those of the European – a different Way, involving different criteria and values. It had simply developed along different lines from ours – different in kind, not in quality nor in degree. Moreover it was, and is, contemporary: not an ancient survival, arrested in development, nor radically confined through mental retardation.

It is this point which we are apt to forget, as our Western European culture, with its complex organization and its stress on technology and wealth, spreads across the face of the earth, laying waste or absorbing other ideologies and patterns of life. We are apt to forget, too, that other peoples have developed through the centuries, adjusting themselves to their peculiar environment, evolving their own answers to the problems of existence, and finding in them satisfaction and meaning within the framework of human reference.

Through trying to understand the behaviour of others, such as the Australian Aborigines, we come closer to understanding ourselves. Here is a way of life built up by one group of people:

what value have they found in it, what satisfaction, what happiness?

And although the Aborigines are people physically different from us, who possess a culture dissimilar to our own, yet with all that they are human beings with the same basic urges, desires, and requirements as ourselves.

THE AUSTRALIAN FAMILY

In 1967 the Liberal government of Harold Holt began to allow migration from Asia, and in 1973 the Whitlam Labor government set aside race as a factor in migration policy. Labor's Minister for Immigration, Al Grassby, promoted a new vision of a multicultural Australia.

The image we manage to convey of ourselves still seems to range from the bushwacker to the sportsman to the slick city business-man. Where is the Maltese process worker, the Finnish carpenter, the Italian concrete layer, the Yugoslav miner or – dare I say it – the Indian scientist? Where do these people belong, in all honesty, if not in today's composite Australian image? Are they to be non-people – despite their economic contribution to our well-being – because they do not happen to fit the largely American-oriented stereotypes of our entertainment industry? It would seem a mark of national maturity to be able to identify firstly what is essential and distinctive about one's own land and its people, and then to portray it consistently with insight and sympathy.

It is a fact that Australia is now one of the most cosmopolitan societies on earth. It is time that all Australians were encouraged to develop a better understanding of what this implies.

To the average Australian, whether 'old' or 'new', terms like 'assimilation', 'integration', 'homogeneous' or 'pluralistic' society are probably meaningless. The concept I prefer, the 'family of the nation', is one that ought to convey an immediate and concrete image to all. In a family the overall attachment to the common good need not impose a sameness on the outlook or activity of each member, nor need these members deny their individuality and distinctiveness in order to seek a superficial and unnatural conformity.

We might well ask ourselves: what is the Australian way of life? The life styles and values of the suburban housewife in Moonee Ponds, the Italian travel agent in Carlton, the Turkish car factory worker, the Slavic Orthodox priest, or the Aboriginal at Lake Tyers? It is all too easy to overlook the pre-existence in this land of the original Australians, millennia before the advent of us 'white ethnics'. Any theory that fails to accord these people an equal place in the family of our nation is out of the question today and in the future. Likewise other ethnic groups introduced to this land by our migration programs may not be denied an equal place in our future society.

My vision of our society in the year 2000 foreshadows a greatly increasing social complexity, in which the dynamic interaction between the diverse ethnic components will be producing new national initiatives, stimulating new artistic endeavours, and ensuring great strength in diversity.

REBUILD YOUR CONVICT SHIPS

Aboriginal protest became more radical in the 1960s and 1970s. Some Aborigines began to claim that only they had a right to be here. This point of view was put in a lively, humorous way in the Aboriginal musical Bran New Dae (1990), written by Jimmy Chi. The show was created and first performed in Broome, on the north-west coast of Western Australia, an old multicultural community with a population that includes Chinese, Japanese, Aborigines and Europeans. This is one of its songs, 'Nothing I would rather be'.

> WILLIE: There's nothing I would rather be
> than to be an Aborigine
> and watch you take my precious land away.
> For nothing gives me greater joy than to
> watch you fill each girl and boy
> with superficial existential shit.

> [Chorus dance on from the side.]

> CHORUS: Now you may think I'm cheeky
> but I'd be satisfied
> to rebuild your convict ships
> and sail you on the tide.

> WILLIE: I love the way you give me God
> and of course the mining board
> for this of course I thank the lord each day.
> I'm glad you say that land rights wrong
> then you should go where you belong
> and leave me to just keep on keeping on.

> WILLIE AND CHORUS: Now you may think I'm cheeky
> but I'd be satisfied
> to rebuild your convict ships
> and sail you on the tide.

FEMALE AUSTRALIANS

In 1994 four historians argued that women had a different history in Australia from that of men, something the history books had overlooked. This is from the introduction to Creating a Nation *by Patricia Grimshaw, Marilyn Lake, Ann McGrath and Marian Quartly.*

The creation of nations has traditionally been seen as men's business. In the fomenting of revolutions, the forging of new political orders and the fashioning of national identities, men have positioned themselves as the main players. We wish to challenge this view of history, by asserting the agency and creativity of women in the process of national generation. Whether in giving birth to babies, or in refusing to do so, in sustaining families and multicultural communities, creating wealth, shaping a maternalist welfare state or in inscribing the meanings of our experience in culture, women have clearly been major actors in the colonial and national dramas. This book explores the myriad ways in which both women and men, Aboriginal and non-Aboriginal, have contributed to the economic, political and cultural life of the separate colonies and then the nation.

Nationalist mythologies have always been gendered: in Australia the self-conscious elaboration of the national identity has involved the celebration of a particular style of white masculinity embodied in the Australian bushman and updated in such films as *The Man from Snowy River* and *Crocodile Dundee* – a style that was often explicitly defined in opposition to a feminine domesticity and forms of masculine behaviour that were similarly stigmatised and stereotyped. Furthermore, to the extent that nationalism involved an assertion of the rights of man against a demeaning imperial domination, it could come into conflict with a feminist interest in the rights of woman. Australian national stereotypes and mythologising have more recently come to be seen as inappropriate to the variety of cultural traditions and identities deriving from Europe, South America and Asia, which have become influential in Australia, largely since World War II. The tension between the recognition and assertion of sexual, racial and cultural differences, on the one hand, and the assimilationist drive of the nation state with its enshrining of one law and one way of life, on the other, is a major theme of our history.

ALL AUSTRALIANS

In 1991 the Commonwealth Parliament established the Council for Aboriginal Reconciliation to work towards bringing Australians and Aboriginal Australians closer together by the time of the anniversary of Federation in 2001. The Declaration for Reconciliation was written by the novelist David Malouf and the Aboriginal scholar and activist Jackie Huggins. It was subsequently amended. The passage referring to the 'gift of one another's presence' was dropped and the Government did not accept the statement of apology.

Declaration for Reconciliation
Speaking with one voice, we the people of Australia, of many origins as we are, make a commitment to go on together recognising the gift of one another's presence.

We value the unique status of Aboriginal and Torres Strait Islander peoples as the original owners and custodians of traditional lands and waters.

We respect and recognise continuing customary laws, beliefs and traditions.

And through the land and its first peoples, we may taste this spirituality and rejoice in its grandeur.

We acknowledge this land was colonised without the consent of the original inhabitants.

Our nation must have the courage to own the truth, to heal the wounds of its past so that we can move on together at peace with ourselves.

And so we take this step: as one part of the nation expresses its sorrow and profoundly regrets the injustices of the past, so the other part accepts the apology and forgives.

Our new journey then begins. We must learn our shared history, walk together and grow together to enrich our understanding.

We desire a future where all Australians enjoy equal rights and share opportunities and responsibilities according to their aspirations.

And so, we pledge ourselves to stop injustice, address disadvantage and respect the right of Aboriginal and Torres Strait Islander peoples to determine their own destinies.

Therefore, we stand proud as a united Australia that respects this land of ours, values the Aboriginal and Torres Strait Islander heritage, and provides justice and equity for all.

2

Independent Spirit

The classic account of the Australian character was given in 1958 by the historian Russel Ward in The Australian Legend. Independence was one of the characteristics he identified. He saw it operating first in convicts and ex-convicts working 'up the country' or in the bush. According to Ward this ethos spread to the rest of the society from the 1890s when the feats of the bushmen were celebrated in the new national literature, particularly in the writings of Henry Lawson and Banjo Paterson. Extracts from their work appear later in this collection. The self-confidence and independence of the men working in the bush were certainly noted by many observers, but other people were also seen to have an independent spirit. The extracts that follow contain some suggestions as to why this was so, and unlike Ward they do not relate the independent spirit to the convict origins of the workforce.

BUSHMEN HAVE IT

John Sidney was a squatter in the far west of New South Wales. He wrote of bush workers and of workers entertaining bosses in A voice from the far interior of Australia (1847).

Good wages and plenty of food, with something perhaps in the climate, render our labourers clever, cute as Yankees, ready to learn anything – as different as possible from the dull, depressed creatures to be found in Buckinghamshire and Dorsetshire.

Often and often, when chilled by the frigid, cautious civility that meets a stranger at every turn in civilized England, do I recall the warm, the hearty, hospitality of these dwellers in the woods; how, after a weary day's journey, they have received me into their huts, spread before me the best fare they could afford; pressed me to stay as many days as would recruit me and my horse; when I departed insisted on refilling my tea-bag and tobacco pouch, if they chanced to be exhausted; and, if by so doing they could put me on a nearer track, they have mounted and ridden ten or fifteen miles on the way with me.

*

The English radical writer Francis Adams visited Australia for a few years in the 1880s (he was trying to stave off tuberculosis). He wrote of the bush-man in the Fortnightly Review *of August 1891 and in* The Australians *(1893).*

The one powerful and unique national type yet produced in Australia is, I have asserted, that of the Bushman.

The smaller resident or squatter or manager almost always shows signs of him: sometimes is merely a slightly refined or outwardly polished form of him.

The selector comes nearer to him still, so near as often to seem almost identic, yet a fine but unmistakable shade of difference severs him from the true Bushman, the Bushman pure and simple, the man of the nation.

It is, then, in the ranks of the shearers, boundary riders, and general station hands, that the perfected sample must be sought.

...

Behold, then, this native-born Australian of the Interior of the first and second generations, sullen and sombre-souled, everlastingly confronting a hostile sun, his digestion ruined with an endless stream of tannin (he calls it tea), a spare eater, precociously and neurotically amorous, biliously and satanically proud, able to shoot rabbits and birds with a rifle, and to sit any horse yet born from morning till night. He cares so little for the curse of existence that on occasion he will grinningly throw away his life for a trifle. When he begins to 'blow' or to swear, his drawling words, super-human lies or face-whipping curses, come out of him in one long, nervous spasm. The English condemnatory volubility is utterly gone.

Four hundred miles inland, where rain sometimes does not fall for two, three, four, or even five years, and then suddenly comes down like a watery avalanche, we shall find no easy human optimism at the very best of times. Nature is hard and cruel, most sinister even when most lovely, and a black rumination, a jesting and pessimistic stoicism, is the sign-manual of the genuine Bushman. Americans will understand this. A life in many ways similar has produced a somewhat similar type, celebrated in history under the name of Abraham Lincoln and the quiet grimness of Ulysses Grant. The melancholy of the bush is an influence which, once thoroughly established, is never shaken off. Yet the bush is the heart of the country, the real Australian Australia, and it is with the Bushman that the final fate of the nation and race will lie.

NEWCOMERS HAVE IT

The Englishman William Howitt travelled the Victorian goldfields in the 1850s. He reported in Land, Labour and Gold (1855) that he was not always treated as he expected a gentleman should be.

A great number of diggers had made a cricket-ground of the highway. They had put down their stumps in the very centre of it, and would neither give pause nor give way for any one. We managed to avoid the flying balls as well as we could. On returning, the same scene was going on, though the mounted police, whose duty it was to have put a stop to this dangerous play in the main road, had just ridden by. As we came up a fellow flung the ball close past my horse's ear, and it was struck back, with furious force, in the direction of Alfred, and it was all that he could do to avoid its striking him in the face. We stopped and quietly remonstrated with them on the danger of their playing in the public road, observing to them, that the ball striking a horse might occasion some very serious accident to the rider. Instead of receiving the observation well, they began to hoot and bawl, and threaten all sorts of things, saying, 'Get along with you; we do as we like here. You are not in England, remember.'

The common people who have come out here seem to delight in this churlish sort of conduct. I verily believe they take it for a sign of independence; but whatever they take it for, they certainly indulge themselves in it most thoroughly. Courtesy is a thing which you might suppose cost something; but I dare say it is, in many cases, only taking their change out of the servility they have been compelled to practise at home. Every man is here his own master; but it will require some time to enable him to become master of himself. This most unattractive and unloveable manner has a very extensive prevalence here, both in town and country, in stores and inns, as well as in huts and on the road-side. I hate servility, but I just as much dislike churlishness; but it requires some refinement of mind to practise and to take a pleasure in courtesy; and a vast mass of the poor devils, male and female, who have come out here, knew no better at home, though they were held in more restraint there.

WOMEN HAVE IT

The English novelist Anthony Trollope arrived in Australia in July 1871 and remained for a year. He came to visit his son who was a squatter in New South Wales but he travelled widely through the colonies. On his return to London he published his impressions of Australia and New Zealand (1873).

Whether men and women dine at five or at seven, whether they drive out regularly or irregularly, whether they hunt foxes or kangaroos, drink bad wine or good, matters little, in regard to social delights, in comparison with the character, the manners, and the gifts of the men and women themselves. In describing Victorians of the upper classes, and of the two sexes, I would say that both in their defects and their excellences they approach nearer to the American than to the British type. And in this respect the Victorian is distinct from the colonist of New South Wales, who retains more of the John-Bull attributes of the mother country than his younger and more energetic brother in the South. This is visible, I think, quite as much in the women as in the men. I am speaking now especially of those women whom on account of their education and position we should class as ladies; but the remark is equally true to all ranks of society. The maid-servant in Victoria has all the pertness, the independence, the mode of asserting by her manner that though she brings you up your hot water, she is just as good as you, – and a good deal better if she be younger, – which is common to the American 'helps'. But in Victoria, as in the States, the offensiveness of this, – for us who are old-fashioned it is in a certain degree offensive, – is compensated by a certain intelligence and instinctive good-sense which convinces the observer that however much he may suffer, however heavily the young woman may tread upon his toes, she herself has a good time in the world. She is not degraded in her own estimation by her own employment, and has no idea of being humble because she brings you hot water. And when we consider that the young woman serves us for her own purposes, and not for ours, we cannot rationally condemn her. The spirit which has made this bearing so common in the United States, – where indeed it is hardly so universal now as it used to be, – has grown in Victoria and has permeated all classes. One has to look very closely before one can track it and trace it to be the same in the elegantly equipped daughter of the millionaire who leads the fashion in Melbourne, and in the little housemaid; – but it is the same. The self-dependence, the early intelligence, the absence of reverence, the contempt for all weakness, – even feminine weakness, – the indifference to the claims of age, the bold self-assertion, have sprung both in the one class and in the other from the rapidity with which success in life has been gained.

CAN LADIES HAVE IT?

'Uncle said he was glad to see I had the spirit of an Australian ... Grannie remarked that I might have the spirit of an Australian, but I had by no means the manners of a lady.' So Sybylla Melvyn is described in My Brilliant Career (1901), the semi-autobiographical novel by Miles Franklin, the pen-name of Stella Franklin, who completed the book before she was twenty-one. Sybylla hated life on her parents' dairy farm. She wanted to be a writer and she did not want to marry. She was delighted to escape to the pastoral property of her grandmother where she was briefly engaged to a neighbouring squatter, Harold Beecham.

'Mr Beecham, I'll trouble you to explain yourself. How dare you lay your hands upon me?'

'Explain!' he breathed rather than spoke, in a tone of concentrated fury. 'I'll make *you* explain, and I'll do what I like with you. I'll touch you as much as I think fit. I'll throw you over the fence if *you* don't explain to *my* satisfaction.'

'What is there that I can explain?'

'Explain your conduct with other men. How dare you receive their attentions and be so friendly with them!'

'How dare you speak to me like that! I reserve the right of behaving as I please without your permission.'

'I won't have the girl with my engagement-ring on her finger going on as you do. I think I have a right to complain, for I could get any amount of splendid women in every way to wear it for me, and behave themselves properly too,' he said fiercely.

I tossed my head defiantly, saying, 'Loose your hold of me, and I'll quickly explain matters to my own satisfaction and yours, Harold Beecham.'

He let me go, and I stepped a pace or two away from him, drew the costly ring from my finger, and, with indifference and contempt, tossed it to his feet, where the juice of crushed strawberries was staining the ground, and facing him, said mockingly –

'Now, speak to the girl who wears your engagement-ring, for I'll degrade myself by wearing it no more. If you think I think you as great a catch as you think yourself, just because you have a little money, you are a trifle mistaken, Mr Beecham, that is all. Ha! ha! ha! So you thought you had a right to lecture me as your future slave! Just fancy! I never had the slightest intention of marrying you. You were so disgustingly conceited that I have been attempting to rub a little of it out of you. Marry you! Ha! ha! Because the social laws are so arranged that a woman's only sphere is marriage, and because they endeavour to secure a man who can give them a little more ease, you must not run away with the idea that it is yourself they are angling for, when you are only the bothersome appendage with which they would have to put up, for the sake of your property. And you must not think that because some women will marry for a home they all will. Go and get a beautiful woman to wear your ring and your name. One that will be able to say yes and no at the right time; one who will know how to dress properly; one who wouldn't for the world do anything that women did not also; one who will know where to buy the best groceries and who will readily sell herself to you for your wealth. That's the sort of woman that suits men, and there are plenty of them; procure one, and don't bother with me. I am too small and silly, and have nothing to recommend me. I fear it speaks little for your sense or taste that you ever thought of me. Ta-ta, Mr Beecham,' I said, over my shoulder with a mocking smile, and walked away.

NED KELLY EMBODIED IT

'Game as Ned Kelly' is an Australian saying. Kelly was the last and most famous of the bushrangers. Bushrangers did rob (and not just from the rich) and murder, but even in their own time they elicited admiration from respectable people. Now Ned Kelly is widely revered and is the best known character in Australian history. In October 1878 Kelly and his gang shot dead four policemen who were hunting for them. Three of the gang died when the police surrounded them twenty months later at Glenrowan. Kelly was captured, and tried for the murder of one of the policemen. He was found guilty and condemned to death by Justice Redmond Barry. As Barry proceeded to pass sentence on him, Kelly interrupted.

HIS HONOUR: Edward Kelly, the verdict is one which you must have fully expected.

PRISONER: Under the circumstances, I did expect this verdict.

HIS HONOUR: No circumstances that I can conceive could here control the verdict.

PRISONER: Perhaps if you had heard me examine the witness, you might understand. I could do it.

HIS HONOUR: I will even give you credit for the skill which you desire to show you possess.

PRISONER: I don't say this out of flashness. I do not recognize myself as a great man; but it is quite possible for me to clear myself of this charge if I liked to do so. If I desired to do it, I could have done so in spite of anything attempted against me.

HIS HONOUR: The facts against you are so numerous and so conclusive, not only as regards the offence which you are now charged with, but also for the long series of criminal acts which you have committed during the last eighteen months, that I do not think any rational person could have arrived at any other conclusion. The verdict of the jury was irresistible, and there could not be any doubt about its being a right verdict. I have no right or wish to inflict upon you any personal remarks. It is painful in the extreme to perform the duty which I have now to discharge, and I will confine myself strictly to do it. I do not think that anything I could say would aggravate the pain you must now be suffering.

PRISONER: No; I declare before you and my God that my mind is as easy and clear as it possibly can be. (Sensation.)

HIS HONOUR: It is blasphemous of you to say so.

PRISONER: I do not fear death, and I am the last man in the world to take a man's life away. I believe that two years ago, before this thing happened, if a man pointed a gun at me to shoot me, I should not have stopped him, so careful was I of taking life. I am not a murderer, but if there is innocent life at stake, then I say I must take some action. If I see innocent life taken, I should certainly shoot if I was forced to do so, but I should first want to know whether this could not be prevented, but I should have to do it if it could not be stopped in any other way.

HIS HONOUR: Your statement involves wicked and criminal reflection of untruth upon the witnesses who have given evidence.

PRISONER: I dare say the day will come when we shall all have to go to a bigger court than this. Then we will see who is right and who is wrong. As regards anything about myself, all I care for is that my mother, who is now in prison, shall not have it to say that she reared a son who could not have altered this charge if he had liked to do so.

His Honour then passed sentence of death, and concluded with the usual formula: 'May the Lord have mercy on your soul.'

PRISONER: Yes, I will meet you there.

Ned Kelly was hanged on 11 November 1880; the Judge died twelve days later.

3

Mateship

'Mate' is an English term which came into much wider use in Australia. It was used for a man with whom one worked, then for a workmate who was a close friend. On the gold diggings 'mate' was the common form of address among the diggers. From the late nineteenth century the term 'mateship' was used for a wider loyalty or for the belief that being mates was very important. Mateship was another characteristic that Russel Ward saw as spreading to the wider society from bush workingmen and being adopted by everyone. In 1958, when Ward published his book The Australian Legend Robert Menzies was the prime minister. He did not talk about mateship; the first and most important characteristic of Australians in his eyes was that they were British. Mateship became truly national when it was embraced and celebrated by a conservative prime minister, John Howard (1996–).

WHO IS MY MATE?

John Chandler was a teenager during the Victorian gold rush. His father owned a farm at Preston just north of Melbourne. He made money for the family by carting goods to the goldfields.

I had been home for some time and the wood was all sold, my father had got his crops in, and there was nothing coming in, so I had to go on the roads again. A young man (another runaway sailor) and I started with the two teams. We got loading for a new diggings where a rush had just taken place. It was called Simpson's Ranges. My mate, as we always called one another, did not know how to manage a team any more than a child, and as we had very high loads and the roads were very bad, especially after we left Castlemaine, I had almost to drive the two teams. We could only get along very slow.

We camped near Carisbrook the first night, and in the morning we thought, as we were short of money, instead of buying meat and sardines, we would shoot some quail, which were very plentiful. We always kept our guns loaded as well as our pistols. My mate saw some quail fly over, and he ran to get the gun which was lying on the tarpaulin in the dray. He caught hold of it by the muzzle, and the hammer must have caught in something, for it went off and all the contents passed through his right arm, shattering it all to pieces, and setting fire to his clothes. I ran and tore them all off, and he fainted in my arms. I could do nothing for the time but stand and hold him, for I thought he was dead, and I alone in the bush. I cooeed as loud as I could, for although my clothes, arms, and hands were burned, I felt nothing of it till after. Fortunately, some men were camped about half a mile from our camp, and they had heard the report of the gun, and then my cooee. They thought something was wrong, so they ran down, and helped me to lay the poor fellow down on the tarpaulin, and the other took off his own shirt (which was calico) and tore it into strips, and then we bound up his arm as well as we could. We then got some boughs from the trees and made as soft a place in the dray as we could, and spread the tarpaulin and blankets, and laid him on it. I then started to drive both teams through the bush, with a very bad road, and a wounded man, who was groaning at every step. Although I drove as careful as I could, I could not help the dray shaking him.

When I got to the creek, there were a number of tents, and I enquired if they could tell me if there was a doctor anywhere about.

They told me there was one a little lower down the creek. I went to him and asked him if he would do something for my mate. He said, 'Yes,' but before he would let me bring him into his tent, he asked me how much money I had got. I showed him all I had, which was the £2 I had drew. He took it, and then I conveyed him inside. He washed the arm and then bound it up and put some lotion on his burns, and then showed me how to put the bandages on, and told me to use nothing but cold water, and keep the bandages wet, and take him to the hospital as soon as I could. This was 125 miles through the bush – very bad roads, six days' journey, two teams to drive, a wounded man in great pain, and not a penny in my pocket, and only a small loaf to eat, and no meat or anything else. Before I started, he said his fee was £5, and I must leave him something for the balance. I left him the gun, which was worth £7, but I never saw it any more; for when I went that way again, which was about two months after, the camp had all gone.

I arrived home at Preston late in the evening of the fifth day. My poor horses and I were nearly starved, and my mate was delirious and was singing. When I saw my father I broke down altogether and burst into tears; a thing I had never done before in the presence of anyone. My father immediately borrowed a spring cart and took him to the hospital. They took him in at once, and told him that he would have to get his arm taken off; as it was his right arm, he said he would rather die. They put all that side in a poultice which drew out the inflammation. They extracted the shot and several pieces of bone. His arm was all shrivelled up, about half the bone being left in, but he got better. He was in the hospital about seven months, and he afterwards went to New Zealand. I only heard from him once, and that was about 30 years after.

*

Rolf Boldrewood, the author of Robbery under Arms, wrote 'Shearing in the Riverina' in 1865, which is a revealing account about mateship since it is written from the squatter's point of view.

Mr Gordon had more than once warned a dark sullen-looking man that he did not approve of his style of shearing. He was temporarily absent, and on his return found the same man about to let go a sheep whose appearance, as a shorn wool-bearing quadruped, was painful and discreditable in the extreme.

'Let your sheep go, my man,' said Gordon, in a tone which somehow attracted the attention of nearly all the shearers, 'but don't trouble yourself to catch another!'

'Why not?' said the delinquent, sulkily.

'You know very well why not!' replied Gordon, walking closely up to him, and looking straight at him with eyes that began to glitter, 'you've had fair warning. You've not chosen to take it. Now you can go!'

'I suppose you'll pay a man for the sheep he's shorn?' growled out the ruffian.

'Not one shilling until after shearing. You can come then if you like,' answered Gordon, with perfect distinctness.

The cowed bully looked savagely at him; but the tall powerful frame and steady eye were not inviting for personal arbitration of the matter in hand. He put up his two pairs of shears, put on his coat and walked out of the shed.

Having arrayed himself for the road he makes one more effort for a settlement and some money wherewith to pay for board and lodging on the road. Only to have a mad carouse at the nearest township, however; after which he will tell a plausible story of his leaving the shed on account of Mr Gordon's temper, and avail himself of the usual free hospitality of the bush to reach another shed. He addressed Mr Gordon with an attempt at conciliation and deference.

'It seems very 'ard, sir, as a man can't get the trifle of money coming to him, which I've worked 'ard for.'

'It's very hard you won't try and shear decently,' retorts Mr Gordon, by no means conciliated. 'Leave the shed!'

Ill-conditioned rascal as the shearer is, he has a mate or travelling-companion in whose breast exists some rough idea of fidelity. He now takes up the dialogue.

'I suppose if Jim's shearing don't suit, mine won't either.'

'I did not speak to you,' answered Mr Gordon, as calmly as if he had expected the speech, 'but of course you can go.'

He said this with an air of studied unconcern, as if he would rather like a dozen more men to knock off work. The two men walk out, but the epidemic does not spread, and several take the lesson home and mend their ways accordingly.

*

In 1922 Carl Strehlow, the Lutheran missionary at Hermannsburg in central Australia, fell ill and left on an epic journey to seek medical help. The journey is described in his son's book Journey to Horseshoe Bend (1969). At one station Mr Buck offered to lend Strehlow some donkeys to pull his buggy through the sand.

After a moment's hesitation, Strehlow accepted with obvious relief and gratitude. 'You are being very good to us, Mr Buck,' he said at last. 'And I'd like to do something for you in return. But I don't know what to offer – please tell me what I could do to show you how grateful I am for your kindness.'

'As you know, Mr Strehlow,' replied Buck, 'us tough bush people in these parts've always had an unwritten law of mateship; and that law says that every man must help everyone else in trouble, never mind whether the poor bugger's been his pal or his enemy. That's the only way us poor bastards up here've been able to survive at all in this tough country. We've no trains, no cars, no doctors, no nurses, and bloody little money. And no man would ever take any money for helping someone that needed his help: he'd only expect to be treated the same way when he needed it himself. Now you're an old friend of the bush people, and you've always been good to Alf and me. There's nothing either of us would accept from you, even if you were in a position to offer us anything.'

UNIONS AND MATESHIP

Mateship was a loyalty to which trade unions appealed to build their strength. Henry Lawson believed in the power of mateship:

> They tramp in mateship side by side –
>   The Protestant and Roman –
> They call no biped lord or sir,
>   And touch their hats to no man!

However, he also recognised the limits to mateship and workers' solidarity in his story 'The Union buries its dead' (1893).

While out boating one Sunday afternoon on a billabong across the river, we saw a young man on horseback driving some horses along the bank. He said it was a fine day, and asked if the water was deep there. The joker of our party said it was deep enough to drown him, and he laughed and rode farther up. We didn't take much notice of him.

Next day a funeral gathered at the corner pub and asked each other in to have a drink while waiting for the hearse. They passed away some of the time dancing jigs to a piano in the bar parlour. They passed away the rest of the time skylarking and fighting.

The defunct was a young Union labourer, about twenty-five, who had been drowned the previous day while trying to swim some horses across a billabong of the Darling.

He was almost a stranger in town, and the fact of his having been a Union man accounted for the funeral. The police found some Union papers in his swag, and called at the General Labourers' Union Office for information about him. That's how we knew. The secretary had very little information to give. The departed was a 'Roman,' and the majority of the town were otherwise – but Unionism is stronger than creed. Liquor, however, is stronger than Unionism; and, when the hearse presently arrived, more than two-thirds of the funeral were unable to follow.

The procession numbered fifteen, fourteen souls following the broken shell of a soul. Perhaps not one of the fourteen possessed a soul any more than the corpse did – but that doesn't matter.

Four or five of the funeral, who were boarders at the pub, borrowed a trap which the landlord used to carry passengers to and from the railway station. They were strangers to us who were on foot, and we to them. We were all strangers to the corpse.

A horseman, who looked like a drover just returned from a big trip, dropped into our dusty wake and followed us a few hundred yards, dragging his packhorse behind him, but a friend made wild and demonstrative signals from a hotel veranda – hooking at the air in front of his right hand and jobbing his left thumb over his shoulder in the direction of the bar – so the drover hauled off and didn't catch up to us any more. He was a stranger to the entire show.

We walked in twos. There were three twos. It was very hot and dusty; the heat rushed in fierce dazzling rays across every iron roof and light-coloured wall that was turned to the sun. One or two pubs closed respectfully until we got past. They closed their bar doors and the patrons went in and out through some side or back entrance for a few minutes. Bushmen seldom grumble at an inconvenience of this sort, when it is caused by a funeral. They have too much respect for the dead.

On the way to the cemetery we passed three shearers sitting on the shady side of a fence. One was drunk – very drunk. The other two covered their right ears with their hats, out of respect for the departed – whoever he might have been – and one of them kicked the drunk and muttered something to him.

He straightened himself up, stared, and reached helplessly for his hat, which he shoved half off and then on again. Then he made a great effort to pull himself together – and succeeded. He stood up, braced his back against the fence, knocked off his hat, and remorsefully placed his foot on it – to keep it off his head till the funeral passed.

A tall, sentimental drover, who walked by my side, cynically quoted Byronic verses suitable to the occasion – to death – and asked with pathetic humour whether we thought the dead man's ticket would be recognized 'over yonder.' It was a G.L.U. ticket, and the general opinion was that it would be recognized.

Presently my friend said:

'You remember when we were in the boat yesterday, we saw a man driving some horses along the bank?'

'Yes.'

He nodded at the hearse and said:

'Well, that's him.'

I thought a while.

'I didn't take any particular notice of him,' I said. 'He said something, didn't he?'

'Yes; said it was a fine day. You'd have taken more notice if you'd known that he was doomed to die in the hour, and that those were the last words he would say to any man in this world.'

'To be sure,' said a full voice from the rear. 'If ye'd known that, ye'd have prolonged the conversation.'

We plodded on across the railway line and along the hot, dusty road which ran to the cemetery, some of us talking about the accident, and lying about the narrow escapes we had had ourselves. Presently someone said:

'There's the Devil.'

I looked up and saw a priest standing in the shade of the tree by the cemetery gate.

The hearse was drawn up and the tail-boards were opened. The funeral extinguished its right ear with its hat as four men lifted the coffin out and laid it over the grave. The priest – a pale, quiet young fellow – stood under the shade of a sapling which grew at the head of the grave. He took off his hat, dropped it carelessly on the ground, and proceeded to business. I noticed that one or two heathens winced slightly when the holy water was sprinkled on the coffin. The drops quickly evaporated, and the little round black spots they left were soon dusted over; but the spots showed, by contrast, the cheapness and shabbiness of the cloth with which the coffin was covered. It seemed black before; now it looked a dusky grey.

I have left out the wattle – because it wasn't there. I have also neglected to mention the heart-broken old mate, with his grizzled head bowed and great pearly drops streaming down his rugged cheeks. He was absent – he was probably 'out back.' For similar reasons I have omitted reference to the suspicious moisture in the eyes of a bearded bush ruffian named Bill. Bill failed to turn up, and the only moisture was that which was induced by the heat. I have left out the 'sad Australian sunset,' because the sun was not going down at the time. The burial took place exactly at midday.

The dead bushman's name was Jim, apparently; but they found no portraits, nor locks of hair, nor any love letters, nor anything of that kind in his swag – not even a reference to his mother; only some papers relating to Union matters. Most of us didn't know the name till we saw it on the coffin; we knew him as 'that poor chap that got drowned yesterday.'

'So his name's James Tyson,' said my drover acquaintance, looking at the plate.

'Why! Didn't you know that before?' I asked.

'No; but I knew he was a Union man.'

It turned out, afterwards, that J.T. wasn't his real name – only 'the name he went by.'

Anyhow he was buried by it, and most of the 'Great Australian Dailies' have mentioned in their brevity columns that a young man named James John Tyson was drowned in a billabong of the Darling last Sunday.

We did hear, later on, what his real name was; but if we ever chance to read it in the 'Missing Friends Column,' we shall not be able to give any information to heart-broken mother or sister or wife, nor to anyone who could let him hear something to his advantage – for we have already forgotten the name.

*

The Shearers Union allowed Aborigines and Maoris to be members, but not Chinese or other Asians. Here is a traditional song about Chinese shearers.

I asked a bloke for shearing down on the Marthaguy.
'We shear non-union here,' he said. 'I call it scab,' said I.
I looked along the shearing-board before I chanced to go,
Saw eight or ten dashed Chinamen all shearing in a row.

CHORUS
It was shift, boys, shift, there was not the slightest doubt
It was time to make a shift with leprosy about.
So I saddled up my horses and whistled to my dog,
And I left that scabby station at the old jig-jog.

MATESHIP: GOOD OR BAD

The historian Miriam Dixson attacked mateship in her 1976 book The Real Matilda.

Australia is internationally renowned as a proud democracy to which one of the world's strongest trade union movements has made crucial contributions. Widely (if hazily) linked in many minds with the strength of our democracy and our unionism is 'mateship'. Mateship is an informal male-bonding institution involving powerful sublimated homosexuality. Indeed some of its most ardent intellectual celebrants are slowly coming to see that mateship is deeply antipathetic to women – even though a major Australian female style is to try and be what I define as 'a matey woman', 'one of the boys'. Notwithstanding these valiant efforts, there is some gut sense in which a woman is not wanted. Back off, don't crowd me, love. You aren't really necessary. You aren't really there.

*

In 2004 four young Australians – Macgregor Duncan, Andrew Leigh, David Madden and Peter Tynan – who had been working in the United States defended mateship in their Imagining Australia: Ideas for Our Future.

In our view, political and social leaders should continue to emphasise the old Australian values when describing the type of country that they envisage for our future, but consciously try to expand the meaning of those values to make them more inclusive for all Australians. As a society, we need to learn how to express the new values of tolerance, compassion and diversity through the language and the values of our history. The reinterpretation of traditional

Australian values will go a long way to overcoming the fear that ordinary people have that diversity and difference is destroying the old Australia, and reassure them that the old values live on strong, albeit in an updated form. The effort to dress up new values in old language is no cynical misrepresentation. Instead, it is a natural way to connect our national dots and make sense of our history and our future. The hope would be that, over time, we will come to regard the essence of being Australian as the commitment to a core set of updated Australian values.

We strongly believe that mateship is a concept ripe to be updated. We should work up the notion of mateship so that, far from being something between blokes, it is used generically within the Australian community to refer to 'good citizenship' and an 'ethic of care' between citizens. It should come to be viewed as the connection that all Australians have between each other, regardless of our background, ethnicity or circumstance, reflecting the humanistic ideals of 'brotherhood', 'fraternity', 'community' and even 'love'. This is what the great Gurindji elder Vincent Lingiari meant when he said, 'we are all mates now', after Gough Whitlam poured red sand into his hands in 1975. We should be proud to call each other 'mate', men and women alike, as young Australians now so freely do. But let us also appreciate that with mateship comes citizenship responsibilities and a duty to respect and care for each other.

4

Diggers

'Diggers' became the Australian term for soldiers in World War I. The origins of the term are uncertain. The commonest explanation is that an officer in France addressed his men as soldiers, and one replied, 'We are not soldiers, we are diggers' – for they spent so much of their time digging and repairing trenches. The name carried with it the democratic ethos of gold diggers of the 1850s. The digger became the most revered national character, and Anzac Day, when the diggers' feats were commemorated, the unofficial national day.

A NATION IS BORN

When Australian soldiers performed so well at the landing at Gallipoli in April 1915, Australians finally threw off the self-doubt about the worth of their nation which arose because not only were they former colonies but convict colonies. The outside doubters they cared most about were the British, so it was important that British experts acknowledged the outstanding feats of their soldiers. The first report of the Gallipoli landing in the Australian newspapers came from an English war correspondent, Ashmead-Bartlett, on 8 May 1915.

The Australians, who were about to go into action for the first time in trying circumstances, were cheerful, quiet and confident. There was no sign of nerves nor of excitement.

As the moon waned, the boats were swung out, the Australians received their last instructions, and men who six months ago had been living peaceful civilian lives had begun to disembark on a strange and unknown shore in a strange land to attack an enemy of a different race.

The boats had almost reached the beach, when a party of Turks, entrenched ashore, opened a terrible fusillade with rifles and a Maxim. Fortunately, the majority of the bullets went high.

The Australians rose to the occasion. Not waiting for orders, or for the boats to reach the shore, they sprang into the sea, and, forming a sort of rough line, rushed at the enemy's trenches.

Their magazines were not charged, so they just went in with cold steel.

It was over in a minute. The Turks in the first trench were either bayoneted or they ran away, and their Maxim was captured.

Then the Australians found themselves facing an almost perpendicular cliff of loose sandstone, covered with thick shrubbery. Somewhere, half-way up, the enemy had a second trench, strongly held, from which they poured a terrible fire on the troops below and the boats pulling back to the destroyers for the second landing party.

Here was a tough proposition to tackle in the darkness, but those colonials, practical above all else, went about it in a practical way.

They stopped for a few minutes to pull themselves together, got rid of their packs, and charged their magazines.

Then this race of athletes proceeded to scale the cliffs without responding to the enemy's fire. They lost some men, but did not worry.

In less than a quarter of an hour the Turks were out of their second position, either bayoneted or fleeing.

But then the Australasians, whose blood was up, instead of

entrenching, rushed northwards and eastwards, searching for fresh enemies to bayonet. It was difficult country to entrench. Therefore they preferred to advance.

WHAT MADE DIGGERS FIGHT?

Australia's military heroes are ordinary soldiers, not generals. Charles Bean, the official historian of Australia's part in World War I, was unusual in dealing closely with the deeds of the soldiers on the front line, and not just the plans and orders of their leaders. At the end of his account of the Gallipoli landing in the Official History, he asked what made the soldiers fight on.

What motive sustained them? At the end of the second or third day of the Landing, when they had fought without sleep until the whole world seemed a dream, and they scarcely knew whether it was a world of reality or of delirium – and often, no doubt, it held something of both; when half of each battalion had been annihilated, and there seemed no prospect before any man except that of wounds or death in the most vile surroundings; when the dead lay three deep in the rifle-pits under the blue sky and the place was filled with stench and sickness, and reason had almost vanished – what was it then that carried each man on?

It was not love of a fight. The Australian loved fighting better than most, but it is an occupation from which the glamour quickly wears. It was not hatred of the Turk. It is true that the men at this time hated their enemy for his supposed ill-treatment of the wounded – and the fact that, of the hundreds who lay out, only one wounded man survived in Turkish hands has justified their suspicions. But hatred was not the motive which inspired them. Nor was it purely patriotism, as it would have been had they fought on

Australian soil. The love of country in Australians and New Zealanders was intense – how strong, they did not realise until they were far away from their home. Nor, in most cases was the motive their loyalty to the tie between Australia and Great Britain. Although, singly or combined, all these were powerful influences, they were not the chief.

Nor was it the desire for fame that made them steer their course so straight in the hour of crucial trial. They knew too well the chance that their families, possibly even the men beside them, would never know how they died. Doubtless the weaker were swept on by the stronger. In every army which enters into battle there is a part which is dependent for its resolution upon the nearest strong man. If he endures, those around him will endure; if he turns, they turn; if he falls, they may become confused. But the Australian force contained more than its share of men who were masters of their own minds and decisions. What was the dominant motive that impelled them?

It lay in the mettle of the men themselves. To be the sort of man who would give way when his mates were trusting to his firmness; to be the sort of man who would fail when the line, the whole force, and the allied cause required his endurance; to have made it necessary for another unit to do his own unit's work; to live the rest of his life haunted by the knowledge that he had set his hand to a soldier's task and had lacked the grit to carry it through – that was the prospect which these men could not face. Life was very dear, but life was not worth living unless they could be true to their idea of Australian manhood. Standing upon that alone, when help failed and hope faded, when the end loomed clear in front of them, when the whole world seemed to crumble and the heaven to fall in, they faced its ruin undismayed.

THE BEST THING AUSTRALIA HAS PRODUCED

The qualities of the digger were summarised in the Round Table in March 1919. This journal of public affairs was produced in London with the aim of strengthening the bonds of empire. Its contributors, who came from all parts of the empire, remained anonymous.

No more original figure than the Australian soldier has appeared in the war. The 'Digger,' as he is affectionately called, is as unique as the 'Poilu' [the French soldier]. Hard to manage in camp, he improved in morale as he neared the firing line. He was fearlessly himself. He behaved in the Strand as he would have done on a Saturday night in the streets of Wagga Wagga. Defiance of convention was his one pose, and he maliciously encouraged the idea, in the conventional among Englishmen, that he was totally lacking in discipline. But there was no body of men who so triumphantly satisfied the supreme test of discipline, the test of being ready in the field just when they were required, and of moving under fire to whatever point they were asked to occupy. The German High Command marked the Australians as First Class Storm Troops. The German lines opposite the Australians had during the last few months to be manned by volunteers. Sir Douglas Haig in his last dispatch gives several 'striking examples of the ascendancy' of the Australians over the German infantry opposite them. The courage of the Australians was not the courage of the savage or the devotee. It was never buoyed up by sentiment or illusion. Its most wonderful feature was a wide-eyed habit of facing things as they really were – of looking at the worst and defying it. The Australian was seldom an optimist. He was always a critic, but he was possessed of a fierce lust to accomplish the job he had been set. This clearness of vision gave him that initiative, that skill under fire, which made up so large a part of his value in the field.

On the human side, few soldiers have had in such measure the supreme soldierly gift of comradeship. Whenever they were in a fight, breaking King's regulations, or raiding the Hun trenches, they stuck together. The Battalion was the digger's home, and he was never truly happy, or a really first-class soldier, away from it. During 1918 an attempt was made to reduce the Brigade organisation by dropping a Battalion. In many cases the idea had to be abandoned owing to the intense feeling aroused in the Battalions that were to lose their identity. The thing, however, that made the Digger the perpetual delight of all who love human nature was his constant play of humour. In this he expressed his soul, his criticism of life, with its wonderful range of insight and feeling, now grotesque, now gay, now grim and sardonic, feeding on the terrible contrasts of the life around him. The 'Digger' is the best thing that Australia has yet produced. She will preserve for ever the memory of this heroic and lovable figure.

ONE DAY OF THE YEAR

The anniversary of the Gallipoli landing became known as Anzac Day after the name of the forces involved, the Australian and New Zealand Army Corps. It was treated as Australia's most solemn holiday. In 1960 the playwright Alan Seymour wrote The One Day of the Year *to be produced at the Adelaide Festival. The organisers rejected it. In the play the young man Hughie refuses for the first time to accompany his father, Alf, to the dawn service on Anzac Day. He and his girlfriend are university students who plan to write a critical article on Anzac Day for the student newspaper with photographs of disgustingly drunken diggers.*

HUGHIE [*swinging on Alf*]: Do you know what you're celebrating today? [*To Mum*] Do you? Do you even know what it all meant?

Have you ever bothered to dig a bit, find out what really happened back there, what this day meant?

MUM: I bin talkin' to Wacka about it just tonight –

HUGHIE: Oh, Wacka – what would he know about it?

ALF: Don't you insult my mate, don't you insult him. He was there, wasn't he?

HUGHIE: What does the man who was there ever know about anything? All he knows is what he saw, one man's view from a trench. It's the people who come after, who can study it all, see the whole thing for what it was –

ALF [*with deepest contempt*]: Book-learnin'. [*Points to Wacka.*] He bloody suffered, that man. You sayin' to me book-learnin' after the event's gunna tell y'more about it than he knows?

HUGHIE: Wacka was an ordinary soldier who did what he was told. He and his mates became a legend, OK. But did any of them ever sit down and look at that damn stupid climb up those rocks to see what it meant?

ALF: How do you know so bloody much?

HUGHIE: How do I know? Didn't you shove it down my throat? [*He has plunged over to bookcase against wall, drags out large book.*] It's all here. Encyclopaedia for Australian kids. You gave it to me yourself. Used to make me read the Anzac chapter every year. Well, I read it. The official history, all very glowing and patriotic. I read it – enough times to start seeing through it. [*He has been leafing through book, finds the place.*] Do you know what the Gallipoli campaign meant? Bugger all.

ALF [*lunging at him*]: You –

HUGHIE [*dodging him*]: A face-saving device. An expensive shambles. The biggest fiasco of the war. [*He starts to read rapidly.*] 'The British were in desperate straits. Russia was demanding that the Dardanelles be forced by the British Navy and Constantinople taken. The Navy could not do it alone and wanted Army support.'

[*His father by now has stopped weaving groggily and stands watching him, trying to take it in.*] 'Kitchener said the British army had no men available.' [*He looks up.*] So what did they do? The Admiralty, in fact, your great favourite, Dad, Winston Churchill at the Admiralty, *insisted* it be done no matter what the risk. Britain's Russian ally was expecting. So your Mr. Churchill, Dad, big bloated blood-sucker that he was, found the solution. Australian and New Zealand troops had just got to Cairo for their initial training … Untrained men, untried. [*He looks quickly back at book.*] 'Perhaps they could be used.' [*He snaps the book shut.*]

Perhaps. Perhaps they could be pushed in there, into a place everybody knew was impossible to take from the sea, to make the big gesture necessary … to save the face of the British. [*He turns on his father.*] … the British, Dad, the bloody Poms. THEY pushed those men up those cliffs, that April morning, knowing, KNOWING it was suicide.

WACKA [*roused*]: You don't know that. 'Ow could anyone know that?

HUGHIE: You know what it was like. [*Grabs the book open.*] Show them the maps. Show them the photos. A child of six could tell you men with guns on top of those cliffs could wipe out anyone trying to come up from below. And there were guns on top, weren't there, Wacka, weren't there?

ALF [*almost shocked sober*]: More credit to 'em, that's what I say, more credit to 'em, they got up there and dug in.

HUGHIE: Oh yes, great credit to them – if you happen to see any credit in men wasting their lives.

ALF: Well, that's war, that's any war …

HUGHIE [*turning on him*]: Yes, and as long as men like you are fools enough to accept that, to say that, there'll always be wars.

ALF: You're tryin' to drag it down.

HUGHIE: It was doomed from the start, it was a waste! Every

year you still march down the street with that stupid proud expression on your face you glorify the – bloody wastefulness of that day. [*He turns away quickly, sits panting and trembling.*]

ALF [*speechless for a moment, then, furious, he turns to the others*]: They don't care, do they? They don't believe in anything. What'd I tell you? What'd I tell you? The whole country's goin' down the drain.

UNKNOWN SOLDIER: ONE OF US

In the 1960s and 1970s it looked as if the celebration of Anzac Day would die out as the young, like Hughie, refused to honour a war and a war, moreover, fought for the empire. But in the 1990s the young displayed a new enthusiasm for Anzac Day and the pilgrimage to Anzac Cove for the service on 25 April was undertaken by thousands. Prime Minister Paul Keating gave new meaning to the Anzac Legend in his speech at the War Memorial at the interment of an unknown soldier in 1993.

We do not know this Australian's name and we never will. We do not know his rank or his battalion. We do not know where he was born, or precisely how and when he died. We do not know where in Australia he had made his home or when he left it for the battlefields of Europe. We do not know his age or his circumstances: whether he was from the city or the bush; what occupation he left to become a soldier; what religion, if he had a religion; if he was married or single. We do not know who loved him or whom he loved. If he had children we do not know who they are. His family is lost to us as he was lost to them. We will never know who this Australian was.

Yet he has always been among those we have honoured. We know that he was one of the forty-five thousand Australians who died on the Western Front. One of the 416,000 Australians who volunteered for service in the First World War. One of the 324,000 Australians who served overseas in that war, and one of the sixty thousand Australians who died on foreign soil. One of the 100,000 Australians who have died in wars this century.

He is all of them. And he is one of us.

This Australia and the Australia he knew are like foreign countries. The tide of events since he died has been so dramatic, so vast and all-consuming, a world has been created beyond the reach of his imagination. He may have been one of those who believed the Great War would be an adventure too grand to miss. He may have felt that he would never live down the shame of *not* going. But the chances are that he went for no other reason than that he believed it was his duty – the duty he owed his country and his king.

Because the Great War was a mad, brutal, awful struggle, distinguished more often than not by military and political incompetence; because the waste of human life was so terrible that some said victory was scarcely discernible from defeat; and because the war which was supposed to end all wars in fact sowed the seeds of a second, even *more* terrible, war, we might think that this Unknown Soldier died in vain.

But in honouring our war dead as we always have, we declare that this is not true. For out of the war came a lesson which transcended the horror and tragedy and the inexcusable folly. It was a lesson about ordinary people – and the lesson was that they were not ordinary.

On all sides *they* were the heroes of that war: not the generals and the politicians, but the soldiers and sailors and nurses – those who taught us to endure hardship, show courage, to be bold as well as resilient, to believe in ourselves, to stick together. The Unknown Australian Soldier we inter today was one of those who by his deeds proved that real nobility and grandeur belongs not to empires and nations but to the people on whom they, in the last resort, always depend.

That is surely at the heart of the Anzac story, the Australian legend which emerged from the war. It is a legend not of sweeping military victories so much as triumphs against the odds, of courage and ingenuity in adversity. It is a legend of free and independent spirits whose discipline derived less from military formalities and customs than from the bonds of mateship and the demands of necessity. It is a *democratic* tradition, the tradition in which Australians have gone to war ever since.

This unknown Australian is not interred here to glorify war over peace; or to assert a soldier's character above a civilian's; or one race or one nation or one religion above another; or men above women; or the war in which he fought and died above any other war; or one generation above any that has or will come later.

The Unknown Soldier honours the memory of all those men and women who laid down their lives for Australia. His tomb is a reminder of what we have lost in war and what we have gained. We have lost more than 100,000 lives, and with them all their love of this country, and all their hope and energy. We have gained a legend: a story of bravery and sacrifice, and with it a deeper faith in ourselves and our democracy, and a deeper understanding of what it means to be Australian.

It is not too much to hope, therefore, that this Unknown Soldier might continue to serve his country. He might enshrine a nation's love of peace and remind us that, in the sacrifice of the men and women whose names are recorded here, there is faith enough for all of us.

WHY ARE DIGGERS GOOD PEACE-KEEPERS?

Over the past twenty years Australian soldiers have been in regular action but not in conventional wars; they have been peace-keepers or peace-makers in many trouble spots around the globe. That they have performed well is somewhat surprising given the older reputation of Australian soldiers as hell-raisers. In Peacekeeping: challenges for the future *(1993) Peter Kieseker considers why Australian soldiers did well in Somalia.*

It is without doubt that the Australians did an exceptional job in Baidoa. The Australians adopted the principles of war and applied them to peace. They selected and maintained their aim – to protect and support the NGOs [non-government organisations] and the Somali people. They took the initiative when necessary and seized and held ground (in this case the airport) as a safe haven for us all (we could now walk and exercise in safety). But, most importantly, they maintained flexibility in all other areas of support and assistance to the agencies and the people.

The interest which the US marines and the French troops displayed in their own security, by contrast, often compromised the protection provided to the NGOs in Baidoa. There were indeed enemies in the streets of Baidoa: petty criminals armed with knives, persons armed with whatever was at hand setting out for whatever reason to disrupt the rehabilitation process. You cannot stop such activity by hiding behind sandbags at a heavily protected airport as the marines did. Nor does riding around in a jeep that heralds your coming make control possible. But if you are an Australian soldier on foot patrol you are close with the enemy and, when the situation calls for it, engage with him.

The UN peace process has been heavily criticised for failing to recognise the fundamental problems behind Somalia's long enduring woes. The underlying problem is not warlords or lack of security but a consistent abuse of human rights by whatever faction happens to be in power. By opening up dialogue with the reasonable members of the Somali community in Baidoa, the Australians were able in a small but effective way to focus on the human rights question and address it with the means at hand – tangibly through the courts and the auxiliary force, intangibly by listening to all comers, especially the weakest members of society. This was an example of the traditional Australian sympathy for the underdog being put to very good use.

According to the UN directives, the Australians were not required to rebuild warehouses or schools or jails, or help with the town's water supply. The forklift drivers did not have to move containers all over town so that NGOs could have secure stores. The diggers did not have to build playground equipment for the orphanage. They did not have to listen to endless elders and try to arbitrate on domestic issues. They did not have to let the elders come in close to them – they could have kept them at arm's length as the French did. But they did do all these things and more. The Australians were there to 'rebuild a nation' and to do that you need to encourage the nation's people to take the initiative. My personal view is that such civic activities probably made for a more interesting and rewarding time for the soldiers, and I am certain that it endeared them to the Somali people and gained them much kudos with the NGOs.

*

Peter Cosgrove, who led the Australian forces in East Timor, reports on his soldiers in The Spirit of the Digger *(2003).*

I think we carry our national characteristics with us, we don't subordinate any important element of the Australian character in the making and the life of a Digger. For example, we still very much have a sense of social justice which applies not just internally to the army but in our dealings with other people. So I would be amazed if Australian soldiers seeing people of other nations suffering hardship, which they do if they go to an area of operations, they will see people who are down and out, if this doesn't strike a tremendous chord in the Digger's heart.

I can recall in the Oecussi enclave a young Corporal from Support Company 3RAR. These troops were our security force down there and I was down visiting them. I used to visit them on frequent occasions. I was way down in one end of the Oecussi enclave about as remote as you can get and in amongst a group of about 10 or 15 3RAR soldiers when this corporal said: 'Sir, can we get a doctor down here?' And I said: 'Why, are you crook?' He said: 'No, we're alright and we see our doctor or the medico from time to time when we need them but where I am, I'm down right on this little village and there's just us infantry soldiers here and we need a doctor and it's for the locals'. I said: 'Yeah, well I suppose I could look into that but you know we're struggling to get the medical system laid out here in all of East Timor.' I said: 'What's the story?' He answered: 'Well, about a week ago a bloke brought his wife to me because she was in very strong labour and he didn't know what to do and we just got on with it.' I said: 'What do you mean?' He said: 'Well, we delivered the baby.' I said: 'Was that a first for you?' He said: 'Absolutely.' He said in the end it was reasonably uncomplicated, everything worked out OK and baby's alright, the mother's made a good recovery and that's fine. I said: 'Oh good. All's well that ends well.' And he said: 'Yeah but yesterday a lady presented with a breech birth … I'm not real good on those!'

A MILITARY TRADITION

John Birmingham in A Time for War *(2005) ponders the reasons for the growth in regard for the military and interest in Anzac Day.*

Once upon a time I lived at the beach, in Bondi, at the northern or 'Paris end' of the bay. It was my habit to take a drink in the evening at the RSL club nestled at the base of Ben Buckler, the sandstone headland on which the Bondi Golf Club and my old apartment sit. It being an RSL, we would stand each night at six o'clock for the prayer of remembrance. It was always a moving occasion, a strange suspended moment when the pokies and racing channel, the piped music and the drunken bullshitting all fell away. They were a rough-headed crew at North Bondi – less so now that the joint has been renovated – but nobody shirked their duty to haul themselves up and spend some time remembering those who left the beach and never came back. Friends from overseas who witnessed the quiet ceremony never failed to be impressed. One, a poet from Czechoslovakia, had always thought Australians to be a shallow, soulless, materialistic people, but she changed her mind after her first experience of the ode to the fallen among the half-empty schooners and chip packets. Like the historian Ken Inglis she felt the religious tenor of the ceremony. Inglis, writing in the *Age* after Anzac Day 2005, credited the revival and endurance of the Gallipoli commemoration with the appeal of a higher faith and 'ancient certainties to young people who are in search of nourishment for the spirit'. This is the first generation of Australians not expecting the men among them to be summoned to war, and Inglis wondered whether they might be disposed 'all the more powerfully to feel humble, even awe-struck, admiration of those who made, as people used to say, the supreme sacrifice.'

The sort of breathless idolatry that now accompanies every

Anzac Day has not always been the rule, of course. In 1965, on the fiftieth anniversary of the Gallipoli landings, a few hundred of the original diggers travelled to Anzac Cove courtesy of the Australian and Turkish governments. A grand total of four hippies from Australia met them there. That number had swelled to five thousand backpackers by 1990, and now even the threat of a terrorist attack cannot dissuade many more from making the trek each year. Those left behind, on the other hand, can assuage their guilt by attending the ever more popular dawn service and march. The early morning ceremony, once the preserve of a few hundred true believers, has swelled to tens of thousands of observers in the main capital cities each year. It is unusual. Really. Even Americans, who are second to none in the worship of their martial heritage, are routinely astounded by the mass solemnity of Australia's unofficial national day. In 2000, NBC, the official US broadcaster for the Sydney Olympics, devoted one of its high-rotation colour pieces to a documentary on this unexpected facet of the Australian character.

Doubtless the passing of the original Anzacs has created a gathering sense of something like nostalgic urgency around the 25th of April. Where once the day had been little more that a freebie holiday, as the 1980s wore on it seemed to accumulate layers of meaning and historical gravity that would have appalled your average anti-Vietnam demonstrator. In short, it took hold of the national imagination. By Remembrance Day in 1993, when Paul Keating dedicated the Tomb of the Unknown Soldier with one of the finest speeches he, or any other prime minister, has ever made, the transition was complete. The oafish brutes of Alan Seymour's 1960 play *The One Day of the Year* had been cleansed of their sins and deified. In a way the generational gap separating Seymour's damaged, drunken father figure, Alf Cook, and his rebellious son, Hughie, is as vast as that between Hughie's contemporaries and the reverential pilgrims who now make their way to Gallipoli each year.

As powerful as the elegiac feelings of loss and historical abandonment at the passing of the first Anzacs might be, on their own they do not explain the renewed esteem of the military in our core culture, the return of the strong, to steal a phrase from Robert Harvey. If there is an unbreakable link between national culture and strategic culture, the explanation for the renaissance of ADF as an institution probably lies outside the armed forces and their increasing tempo of operations.

In 1992, Paul Kelly released his seminal work *The End of Certainty*, which examined the destruction of the Australian Settlement. The five great pillars of Federation – state paternalism, industry protection, wage arbitration, White Australia and the Empire – have now all been swept away to a greater or lesser degree. The last bastion, comprising the centralised wage system and its protectors in the union movement, faces imminent destruction at the hands of the Commonwealth. The very idea of the state has changed fundamentally. Where once it was thought of as a benevolent guarantor of civil society, the neo-liberal philosophy embraced with varying degrees of enthusiasm by all of the mainstream parties now conceives of government as a mere adjunct to the market, to which most issues of resource allocation are best referred.

Against this background we can see the 'reconnection' of the Australian people to its military as something more than a crude militarisation of national politics.

5

Larrikins

The word 'larrikin' is a dialect word from Britain, which came into widespread use in Australia. A larrikin in Australia was a tough, violent, young troublemaker. It has often been believed that the word originated here when an Irish policeman, describing a young man's offence to a magistrate, said, 'He's been larrrkin' around.' The larrikins operated in groups or pushes and were violent towards each other and to respectable citizens. Over time larrikin lost its hard edge and reverted to something like its original British meaning – 'a mischievous or frolicsome youth' – and could be applied to a man of any age or to an approach to life. Australians are now very ready to indulge a larrikin.

WELL-FED ROUGHS

The journalist John Stanley James was an expert on Melbourne's low-life. His description comes from the Vagabond Papers (1877).

One marked difference between the Melbourne larrikin and his compeers elsewhere is his extreme boldness and contempt of authorities. In Europe, the 'rough' avoids the neighbourhood of police courts. He loves not to be known by magistrates or detectives. But here, the larrikin not only chaffs and annoys the policeman on his beat, but daily crowds the police court, and manifests the liveliest interest in the fate of male or female friends who may be on trial. A youth, or a girl of a certain class being brought in, you will see that their first movement is to peep around the corner of the dock and exchange a wink with their sympathizing 'pals'. Many of the youths who daily crowd the small space allotted to the general public at the police court are known as thieves from their youth upwards; crime is hereditary with them. Another marked difference, which is in the larrikin's favour, is his generally better-fed and better-clothed appearance. The rowdy and thief in the old world, after all, lead a miserable life, and generally their profession does not appear to be a lucrative one; but here, in the first stage, they seem physically in good shape.

It is commonly reputed that a vagrant gets a heavier sentence than a minor thief; if so, it is the better for both of them. Many young larrikins are brought up 'on the vag'. They are known thieves and bad characters, according to the police, who attempt to rid the neighbourhood of them in this way; but as a rule, a subscription is raised which obtains the services of a legal gentleman, who produces evidence to show that his client is a hard-working, respectable youth, and the larrikin is discharged, to the triumph of his companions and discomfiture of 'Mr. Detective'.

TAKE A ROCK AND SMASH THAT WINDER

In 'The Captain of the Push' (1892) by Henry Lawson, the captain examines a new recruit from the bush.

> 'Now, look here,' exclaimed the captain to the stranger from
>   the bush,
> 'Now, look here – suppose a feller was to split upon the push,
> Would you lay for him and fetch him, even if the traps were
>   round?

Would you lay him out and kick him to a jelly on the ground?

Would you jump upon the nameless – kill, or cripple him, or
 both?

Speak? or else I'll – SPEAK!' The stranger answered, 'My kerlonial oath!'

'Now, look here,' exclaimed the captain to the stranger from
 the bush,

'Now, look here – suppose the Bleeders let you come and join
 the push,

Would you smash a bleedin' bobby if you got the blank alone?

Would you break a swell or Chinkie – split his garret with a
 stone?

Would you have a "moll" to keep yer – like to swear off work
 for good?'

'Yes, my oath!' replied the stranger. 'My kerlonial oath! I
 would!'

'Now, look here,' exclaimed the captain to that stranger from
 the bush,

'Now, look here – before the Bleeders let yer come and join the
 push,

You must prove that you're a blazer – you must prove that you
 have grit

Worthy of a Gory Bleeder – you must show your form a bit –

Take a rock and smash that winder!' And the stranger, nothing loth,

Took the rock and – smash! They only muttered, 'My kerlonial
 oath!'

So they swore him in, and found him sure of aim and light of
 heel,

And his only fault, if any, lay in his excessive zeal;
He was good at throwing metal, but we chronicle with pain
That he jumped upon a victim, damaging the watch and chain
Ere the Bleeders had secured them; yet the captain of the push
Swore a dozen oaths in favour of the stranger from the bush.

REFORMED BY LOVE

In his best-selling The Songs of a Sentimental Bloke (1915) C.J. Dennis tells of a larrikin's love affair and marriage with Doreen, which led to his reformation. The glossary of larrikin words below is as provided in the first edition. These are verses from the song 'Doreen' in which the larrikin declares he has 'done me dash', that is, he will give up the larrikin life for his love.

'Er eyes! Soft in the moon, such boshter eyes!
    'An when they sight a bloke … O, spare me days!
'E goes all loose inside; such glamour lies
    In 'er sweet gaze.
It makes 'im all ashamed uv wot 'e's been
    To look inter the eyes of my Doreen.

The wet sands glistened, an' the gleamin' moon
    Shone yeller on the sea, all streakin' down.
A band was playin' some soft, dreamy choon;
    An' up the town
We 'eard the distant tram-cars whir an' clash.
An' there I told her 'ow I'd done me dash.

'I wish't yeh meant it,' 'Struth! And did I, fair?
    A bloke 'ud be a dawg to kid a skirt

Like 'er. An' me well knowin' she was square.
     It 'ud be dirt!
'E'd be no man to point wiv 'er, an' kid.
I meant it honest; an' she knoo I did.

She knoo. I've done me block in on 'er, straight.
     A cove 'as got to think some time in life
An' get some decent tart, ere it's too late,
     To be 'is wife.
But, Gawd! 'Oo would 'a' thort it could 'a' been
My luck to strike the likes of 'er … Doreen!

Aw, I can stand their chuckin' off, I can.
     It's 'ard; an' I'd delight to take 'em on.
The dawgs! But it gets that way wiv a man
When 'e's fair gone.
She'll sight no stoush; an' so I 'ave to take
Their mag, an' do a duck fer 'er sweet sake.

Fer 'er sweet sake I've gone and chucked it clean:
     The pubs an' schools an' all that leery game.
Fer when a bloke 'as come to know Doreen,
     It ain't the same.
There's 'igher things, she sez, for blokes to do.
An' I am 'arf believin' that it's true.

     …

Block – The head. To lose or do in the block – To become flustered;
    excited; angry; to lose confidence
Bloke – A male adult of the genus homo
Boshter – Adjective expressing the superlative of excellence
Break – To depart in haste
Chuck up – To relinquish. Chuck off – To chaff; to employ sarcasm

Clean – Completely; utterly

Cove – A 'chap' or a 'bloke'

Dash, to do one's – To reach one's Waterloo (i.e. final defeat)

Dawg (dog!) – A contemptible person; ostentation

Duck, to do a – See 'break'

Fair – Extreme; positive

Kid, to – to deceive, to persuade by flattery

Leery – Vulgar; low

Mag – To scold or talk noisily

Point, to – To seize unfair advantage; to scheme

School – A club; a clique of gamblers, or others

Sight – To tolerate; to permit; also to see; observe

Skirt – A female

Square – Upright, honest

Stoush – To punch with fist; violence

'Struth – An emaciated oath

Take 'em on – Engage them in battle

Tart – A young woman (contraction of sweetheart)

CENSORED

In 1915 Australian soldiers in larrikin mode trashed the red light district – the Wazzir – of Cairo before leaving Egypt for Gallipoli. This did not bring credit on Australia. C.J. Dennis wanted to include a justification of the diggers' acts in his Moods of Ginger Mick, in which he celebrated the military exploits of one of the Sentimental Bloke's larrikin mates. The censor banned the song dealing with this incident. Dennis gave it the title 'The Battle of the Wazzir'.

It was part of their native carelessness; an' part their native skite;

Fer they kids themselves they know the Devil well,
'Aving met 'im, kind uv casu'l, on some wild Australian night –
    Wine an' women at a secon'-rate 'otel.
But the Devil uv Australia 'e's a little woolly sheep
To the devils wot the desert children keep.

So they mooches round the drink-shops, an' the Wazzir took
    their eye,
    An' they found old Pharoah's daughters pleasin' Janes;
An' they wouldn't be Australian 'less they give the game a fly …
    An' Egyp' smiled an' totted up 'is gains.
'E doped their drinks, an' breathed on them 'is aged evil
    breath …
    An' more than one woke up to long fer death.

When they wandered frum the newest an' the cleanest land
    on earth,
    An' the filth uv ages met 'em, it was 'ard.
Fer there may be sin an' sorer in the country uv their birth;
But the dirt uv centuries ain't in the yard.
They was children, playin' wiv an asp, an' never fearin' it,
An' they took it very sore when they wus bit.

'Ave yeh seen a crowd uv fellers takin' chances on a game,
    Crackin' 'ardy while they thought it on the square?
'Ave yeh 'eard their owl uv anguish whey they tumbled to the
    same,
    'Avin' found they wus the victims uv a snare?
It was jist that sort uv anger when they fell to Egyp's stunt;
An', remember, they wus trainin' fer the front.

EXCUSED BY WAR

The Twenty Thousand Thieves (1951) by Eric Lambert tells of the exploits of Australian soldiers in North Africa in World War II. Captain Henry Gilbertson and Lieutenant Ken Crane discuss how to deal with the larrikin soldier Dooley Franks. Tommy Collins, another larrikin, reflects on the advantages of wearing the uniform.

'Let's talk about Dooley Franks. All I have here is this major's written account. What really happened?'

'Probably everything the major's written, if I know Franks. However, I've had a talk with Lucas and Gribble – Franks's section corporal.'

'They were there?'

'Gribble was.'

'What's the story?'

'To begin with, they were geligniting fish, which is against orders. This major appeared on the scene and told them to cease forthwith. Franks, it seems, told him to mind his own bloody business, that they were Australians and no concerns of any stray officer of the British army.'

Henry grinned: 'Or words to that effect?'

'Yes. You can imagine the sort of embellishments that a man like Franks would provide. Well, the major demanded to know their names and numbers. Franks demanded to see the major's pay-book and identification first.'

'Did he?' Henry hooted with laughter. 'He was quite within his rights, you know. After they caught those two Huns masquerading as Poles the Divisional Commander laid it down that all ranks had to identify themselves on demand.'

'Well, the major wouldn't. Franks promptly denounced him as a spy, pushed him into the sea and hit him in the face with a dead fish as he rose to the surface. The others pelted him with fish and stones. He had to swim a hundred yards along the shore to escape them. Is that the major's story?'

'More or less. He doesn't put it quite so humorously as you. Who else was there?'

'Cain, Perkins, Brett, Gribble, Collins. By the way, Gribble tells me he tried to restrain them, and took no part in the pelting. He asked me to make this clear, which I promised to do.'

'Gribble? That's the man who still polishes his boots.'

Crane took the remark as ridicule: 'He's got a sense a responsibility. A cut above most of the others, I'm glad to say.'

Henry looked down at his own boots, which the sand had worn to the color of blotting-paper, and grimaced.

'I wanted,' said Crane, 'to put in a word for him before you do whatever you decide.'

'Ken – I'm going to do precisely nothing.'

'Nothing! But – but this is a serious complaint from a major of the British army!'

'And I am a captain of the Australian army and tomorrow my company goes to Benghazi. What am I to do between now and tomorrow morning? Arrange to have six good men court-martialled and left behind? Franks is the best Bren gunner in this battalion. He handles a Bren as if it were a pistol. Just now that's more important to me than all the majors in the British army.'

...

Tommy Collins lay in Two Section's strong-post and decided that if he didn't get out of Tobruk soon he would go mad. It hadn't been too bad when the Easter battles were on. You'd had no time to think then and it gave you a chance to prove you had guts – which was important to Tommy, for he valued personal courage highly. But now, with only an occasional skirmish, a man had time to get bored – and remember.

Up till now the army had meant freedom for Tommy. For the first time in his life he had got drunk, accosted women, started fights, without keeping one eye over his shoulder for a policeman. Somehow the war seemed to have licensed drunkenness and the pursuit of women: as long as you wore a uniform no-one seemed surprised at what you did. His week-end leaves in Sydney, his excursions to Jaffa and Tel Aviv had been wild and free, and for the first time he felt himself to be living fully. Women and drink were plentiful and cheap; always on hand was the answer to a sudden lust. Yes, back among the flesh-pots Tommy had been grateful for the uniform which made him liked and tolerated.

For the hundredth time he cursed the bravado that had made him join the infantry.

A LARRIKIN IN THE LODGE

Two prime ministers were often described as larrikins or having a larrikin streak, John Gorton (Liberal 1967–70) and Bob Hawke (Labor 1983–91). The political scientist Sol Encel examines 'The Larrikin Leaders' in Nation, 25 May 1968.

The figure of the larrikin is prominent in Australian social and cultural history, but he has not been treated so far as a political phenomenon. Yet there must be many people who can readily identify acts or persons on whom the label can appropriately be hung.

The word itself first appeared in the public prints about 1870, and had become part of Standard English by the early years of this century. Its exact derivation has always been controversial, but its synonyms are widely accepted: flash, tough, irreverent, rowdy. The same characteristics, adapted to the special needs of the political arena, appear in the political larrikin: they include a talent for making speeches laced with bar-room humour, a contempt for ideas or ideals in politics, a palpable liking for the so-called 'cut and thrust' of parliamentary debate, and a general lowbrow stance. Sir Arthur Fadden, one of the more likeable of larrikin types in Federal politics, still enjoys a reputation for earthy stories in Canberra. When his knighthood was elevated from K.C.M.G. to G.C.M.G., he is reported to have said, 'Not bad – twice a (k)night at my age.' Of a Country Party colleague who had remarried at an advanced age, he is said to have observed that the bridegroom's present to the bride would be an antique pendant.

George Reid, a one-time premier of New South Wales, fourth Prime Minister of Australia, and first High Commissioner in London, enjoyed a similar reputation both on the hustings and in parliament. One of the fattest men to be prominent in politics, he used his girth as a regular basis for repartee, and his ever-present monocle as a prop. When another stout member of the state parliament complained to the Speaker that attendance at an important debate was very thin, Reid rose and drawled: 'It will never be a thin House while the honourable member and I sit in it.' Serious politics bored him. When the House of Representatives was debating an important Bill which he had introduced as Prime Minister, the Leader of the Opposition, Alfred Deakin, hit on an ingenious method of cutting the debate short. He persuaded his followers to refrain from interjecting during Reid's speech. Bored by the absence of the usual repartee on which he thrived, Reid lost interest and sat down prematurely, giving the Opposition a field day.

The strain of larrikinism in Australian politics may readily be seen as a response to its wider importance in Australian society as a whole. If politicians at the summit of their careers go on behaving like larrikins, they are clearly gaining some response from their public by doing so.

6

Suburban Nation

*Australia was described by Donald Horne in The Lucky Country (1964)
as the first suburban nation. From early on a high proportion of the population lived in cities and most city-dwellers did not live in the town centre;
they occupied houses standing in their own ground in the suburbs. In the
1950s, when home building and home ownership boomed, critics of the
narrow conformity of Australian life saw the suburb as symbol and cause
of it.*

A CALAMITY

*The architectural historian Robin Boyd gives the history and significance
of Australia's Home (1952).*

This is the story of a material triumph and an aesthetic calamity.

Towards the end of the eighteenth century, Englishmen began
building houses on the east coast of this warm land of curious life
and unknown vastness. They had selected, more by luck than explo-
ration, the banks of a magnificent harbour, a place which posterity
generally recognized as one of the best sites in the world.

It was about four centuries after the great community hall of
the mediaeval manor house began to break into a collection of
private rooms, and one and a half centuries before each collection
of private rooms began to melt back into a single living space. It

was two centuries after Queen Elizabeth had proclaimed the principle of a private house for every family. It was midway in history between Inigo Jones and Le Corbusier.

These Englishmen, marines and convicts, and their few women, had left the England of the Adam brothers; of tall, pastel-tinted rooms, gilded ornament and gleaming silverware; of Wedgwood and the water-closet – a state where domestic building for the privileged had reached physical and artistic maturity. Many of them, not having been privileged, knew nothing of these things. But all of them had the acquired English taste for privacy, and it was this taste which remained a prime motive through the subsequent generations of home-building.

Each family asked, when the day's work was done, for isolation from the next family. Each member asked for the possibility of privacy from the remainder of the family. The nation was built on the principle that for every family there should be a separate house and for every person there should be a separate room.

The pattern of this culture, through the years and across the great distances, was fairly consistent. Each town was in essence a great sea of small houses around a commercial and industrial island. Each house was a group of compartments of varying size, each compartment serving a slightly different purpose. People cooked in one, ate in another, sat reading in another, tucked their children to bed in another, slept in another. There came a time when they performed the principal movements of the preparation for the day – shave, tooth-clean, toilet, shower and dress – in four different cubicles. They liked to have separate compartments for eating breakfast and dinner, and if possible a third for lunch. They liked one room for sitting by themselves and one for sitting with visitors.

In a land of rolling plains and wide blue skies, a race of cheerful agoraphobes grew up in little weather-sealed boxes. By the middle of the twentieth century, with the population just over eight million, Australia had nearly two million private houses with an average of five rooms each – more rooms than people. And of every ten people, five lived in a capital city, one other lived in a city of more than 12,500 inhabitants, and another lived in a big town; only about three lived in a non-urban area. Living in an urban area almost invariably meant living in a suburban area. In 1947 (census year) 93.5 per cent of Sydney's 1,484,434 inhabitants lived outside the municipality of Sydney, and 92 per cent of Melbourne's 1,226,923 lived outside the city in the vast ring of suburbs.

The suburb was the major element of Australian society. Factory, shop, office, theatre and restaurant were not radically different the world over. The interior of an Australian house could be given any atmosphere; it might be no different from the interior of an apartment in Rome or a flat in Regent's Park, London. But in the suburb was experienced that essentially Australian part of town life which lay between work and home.

It was 'Sunday Sport Not Allowed', 'Keep Off the Grass', 'Dogs Found Will Be Destroyed', 'Commit No Nuisance', and countless other kindred elements of a half-world between city and country in which most Australians lived.

SUBURBAN REBELLION

In My Brother Jack (1964), the best-selling novel by George Johnston, the narrator, David Meredith, falls out with his wife over what should be planted in their suburban garden.

When I got back to Beverley Grove I dumped the sapling on the drive near the front gate and went through to the kitchen and Helen said, 'David, where on earth have you been? You didn't say you were going somewhere. I thought you were still up there on the roof, and when I went to call you for your cup of tea –'

'I went out and bought a tree,' I said.

'A *tree*?'

'A tree for the garden. I drove down to Goodenough's Nurseries. Only six bob.' I added proudly.

'David, how marvellous!' she cried. 'Where is it?'

'Out the front. Come and see.'

Her expression changed when she did see it, and admittedly it did look rather scruffy and limp and drab with its roots packed up into a big shapeless pudding of wet hessian.

'Yes, but what is it?' she asked. 'It – it looks like a gum-tree.'

'It *is* a gum-tree. It's a sugar-gum.'

'Oh,' she said, and for a moment or two she looked blank, and then, 'Where are you going to put it?' she said. 'I mean, where do you want it to grow?'

'There.' I pointed. 'Right there, smack bang in the middle of the lawn!'

'Oh!'

'Why do you just keep saying "Oh"?'

'No reason … I mean, well, do you really think that's the place for it, David? I mean, if it's to be there, right in the middle of everything, I would have thought something smaller, or even –'

'What's wrong with a gum-tree?'

'Well, if you want to know, darling, I personally think they're rather *ordinary*. They're so drab, David. I'd honestly prefer something decorative, especially for there, right in the front of the house, some nice flowering shrub, or camellia, or mock-orange. What *would* look lovely would be one of those Japanese dwarf-maples.'

'Not on your sweet life, my dear! No dwarf anythings! I want a tree. A proper bloody tree! Do you realise,' I said, 'there's not one tree growing in this whole damned street … on the whole estate if it comes to that? And this is a *grove* we live in, darling. It's printed on the footpath at the corner. Beverley Grove. Don't you know the definition of a grove? We've been letting them pull the wool over our eyes. The Beverley – Park – Gardens – Estate.' I spaced the words with careful sarcasm. 'It isn't a park and it isn't a garden and this isn't a grove. They've got us here on false pretences. They can't bloody well do that to *us*! Besides, this is our chance to be original. Let *us* be leaders of fashion, Helen. And let me point out – because old Goodenough told me this himself – that this thing you're turning up your nose at – all right, I admit it *does* look a bit scraggy at the moment – but he assured me it'll grow into a tree forty feet high in two years. A *real tree*! And what this damned place needs is a good firm far-sighted policy of reafforestation!'

I went round to the shed in the back yard then and got out the pick and shovel.

Old Joe Goodenough had been right – it took astonishingly. One could almost see it grow. At some stage I must have accepted that this tree had become very much more than merely a symbol of protest against suburban values. If I had not, in fact, planted it with malice aforethought, I very soon began to be aware that I was using it as a weapon with which to force a situation which I was not prepared to attack directly. I gave it much attention, forking, watering, manuring, – far more attention than I would give to the now-hated flower-beds which were Helen's pride and joy. (One was always on the prowl, of course, trying to sniff out other sources of resentment.) It even came to the absurdly childish point where I would water the tree copiously and, in the case of a eucalypt quite unnecessarily, and deliberately neglect those beds which I had come to detest because of the little wooden label-stakes which Helen had lettered herself so neatly. I think I really hated them because of the affectation she had perpetrated in using only the botanical names for her flowers, and I would stalk the hated beds at dusk, spitting the words out under my breath: *Phlox Drummon-dii, Tropæolum, Arctotis, Myosotis dissitiflora, Antirrhinum!* God! what was wrong with forget-me-not or snapdragon?

As it worked out, it was neither Helen nor I who forced the issue in the end, although Helen was obliged to act as the intermediary.

'David, I'm afraid we'll have to do something about that tree in the front.'

'Do what?' I asked.

'Well, what happened is that Mr. Treadwell from next door dropped in here this afternoon. He's complaining about it.'

'He's *what*! It's not *his* bloody tree!'

'He insists you'll have to dig it out. The roots are getting in under the cement of his drive.'

'Oh, bollocks!' I said. 'His drive's thirty feet away from the tree! Do you mean to tell me that roots can go thirty feet underground in a few bloody months!'

'*I'm* not telling you anything, darling. I am simply repeating to you what *he* says. Treadwell is a perfectly nice inoffensive little old man, and he's not a fussy neighbour, and he was most polite about it all. But you know he is a very keen amateur gardener himself and –'

'Well, the old bastard's got nothing *else* to do, has he? He's on a Government pension. He doesn't work. And what the devil has that got to do with our gum-tree?'

'Because he also claims that a tree like that takes the good out of the soil, too – our own lawn *is* getting awfully patchy, darling – and if the roots get near his dahlia beds he –'

'Oh, go to blazes with his dahlia beds. And what's wrong with some upended cement slabs? The place is too damned neat as it is. It's – it's like having some damned woman walking around after you with an ash-tray in her hand, or plumping up the cushions the minute you stand up. My God! I'd like to have two whacking great Moreton Bay figs like those at the Turleys', and then we could tip the slabs up the whole length of the street! Which might be a bloody good thing!'

THE TAMED MALE

In the 1950s Barry Humphries, who became Australia's most famous comic, satirised the suburbs with his leading characters being Edna Everage, the confident and brash wife, and Sandy Stone, the tamed boring husband. Here is Sandy Stone on 'A nice night's entertainment'.

[*Sandy, in pyjamas and dressing gown, is discovered seated in a shabby armchair. He addresses the audience.*]
I went to the R.S.L. the other night and had a very nice night's entertainment. Beryl, that's the wife, came along too. Beryl's not a drinker but she had a shandy. She put in quite a reasonable quantity of time yarning with Norm Purvis's good lady and I had a beer with old Norm and some of the other chappies there. I don't say no to the occasional odd glass and Ian Preston, an old friend of mine, got up and sang a few humorous numbers – not too blue, on account of the womenfolk – so that altogether it was a really nice type of night's entertainment for us both. We called it a day round about ten-ish; didn't want to make it too late a night as Beryl had a big wash on her hands on the Monday morning and I had to be in town pretty early, stocktaking and one thing and another.

Well, we got back to Gallipoli Crescent about twenty past and Beryl and I went to bed.

We were very glad we hadn't made it too late a night on the Sunday because the Chapmans were expecting us over on the Monday night for a couple of hours to look at some slides of their trip.

They're a very nice type of person and some of the coloured pictures he'd taken up north were a real ... picture. Vi Chapman had gone to a lot of trouble with the savouries and altogether it was a really lovely night's entertainment for the two of us. Educational too. Well, round about ten I said we'd have to be toddling. You see, we didn't want to make it too late a night because Tuesday was the Tennis Club picture night and Beryl had a couple of tickets.

Well, there's not much I can say about the Tuesday, except that it was a really lovely night's entertainment. We're not ones for the pictures as a rule but when we do go we like to see a good bright show. After all, there's enough unhappiness and sadness in the world without going to see it in the theatre. Had a bit of strife parking the vehicle – you know what it's like up around that intersection near the Civic. Anyway, we found a possie in the long run just when we were beginning to think we might miss the blessed newsreel. The newsreel had a few shots of some of the poorer type of Italian housing conditions on the Continent and it made Beryl and I realise just how fortunate we were to have the comfort of our own home and all the little amenities round the home that make life easier for the womenfolk, and the menfolk generally, in the home. We left soon after interval as the next show wasn't the best and I was feeling a bit on the tired side. Besides, Beryl was expecting her sister and her husband over for five hundred on the Wednesday and we didn't want to make it too late a night.

So, Beryl and I went to bed.

Had to slip out of the office on the Wednesday lunch hour to get a few cashews to put round the card table. Beryl was running up a batch of sponge fingers with the passionfruit icing. There's no doubt about it, Beryl makes a lovely sponge finger.

Well, the card night went off very nicely indeed, except that Beryl's sister Lorna got a bit excited during the five hundred and knocked over a cup of tea and a curried egg sandwich on the new carpet. Oh, she was very apologetic, but as I said to Beryl later, being sorry won't buy you a new wall-to-wall. And you know what curried egg does to a burgundy Axminster.

By and large though, all things considered, and taking everything into account, it was a pretty nice night's entertainment.

They left early-ish. And Beryl and I went to bed …

WOMEN IN CHARGE

Before women's liberation, men went off to work and women remained at home in the suburb in charge of house and children. This bred stronger women than the women's liberation movement was willing to allow, as Craig McGregor reported in Profile of Australia *(1966).*

The most surprising feature of family life in Australia, for such an overtly masculine nation, is the way the family group is dominated by the mother. Indeed, the Australian family seems to be even more 'mother-centred' than the typical American family. A recent survey found that by far the most common pattern was one in which the mother both made the important family decisions and carried out the important family activities. Taken over all, mothers were responsible for half of all decisions and 40 per cent of all actions, while fathers were responsible for only 2 per cent of decisions and 15 per cent of actions. And joint activities by both parents were fairly rare compared with the amount of independent action taken by either the father or the mother. All this fits in with the everyday evidence about Australian families: the father appears to be the source of authority, but when one of the children wants to do something the reply is often 'Go and ask your mother' or 'If it's all right with Mum, it's all right with me.' Australian fathers take far less part in general family activities than their counterparts in many overseas countries. In America about 90 per cent of fathers take part in virtually all the main regions of family activity, but in Australia hardly any do. Boys and girls both regard their mothers, not their fathers, as the main source of praise and punishment and adolescents have more conflicts with their mothers than their fathers. All this emphasizes the important role of the mother, so that Australian families could well be called a 'matriduxy' – the mother does not rule, but she certainly leads.

*

In Struggletown (1984) historian Janet McCalman writes on women in working-class Richmond in the first half of the twentieth century.

The working-class family was most commonly a matriarchy where women bore the major responsibility for the expenditure of the family income, the care of the children, the quality of family life. Women sometimes regarded their husbands as one of the children except that they slunk out to play at the pub or with the SP bookie. Battling against poverty bred often formidable middle-aged women who towered over their feckless and immature husbands. The vast majority of men regarded it as a matter of pride that their wives did not have to go to work, and their wives agreed with them: a working wife signalled masculine failure. None the less, men could resent their role as compliant and barely tolerated providers.

*

Novelist Tim Winton remembers the women in his family, as recorded in Good Weekend, *27 August 1994.*

I grew up in an extended family where the matriarchs made all the running. Perhaps it was a genetic hiccup, but the women made all the plays and the men followed. The women had more drive about them, they had more of a hardness. They were stronger-willed and altogether more fierce as personalities. Their children feared them into middle age and beyond. I was always more fearful (or at the very least, watchful) of my grandmothers and aunts than their men. Most of them had the tempers and the tongues; they were more vengeful than their men and they were always the final authority. My grandmothers ran their families by sheer force of character, by brilliant organisation and hard work or by mean-spirited sabotage and humiliation. Their husbands, by comparison, were mild and ineffectual.

FREEDOM AND VARIETY

In Ideas for Australian Cities (1970) Hugh Stretton, a leading intellectual, defended suburban living which other intellectuals had mocked. Perhaps the suburbs were not the enemy of the independent spirit.

With good design, that allegedly monotonous and repetitive suburban quarter-acre can include an infinite variety of indoor and outdoor spaces, further increased if some of the partitions are flexible. Large or small, private or open, sunny or cool, paved or overgrown, efficient or romantic, the rooms in the house and the quarters of its garden can offer real variety of colour, use and mood. Suburb-haters, thinking of people without personal resources in ill-designed houses and gardens, too often undervalue the free and satisfying self-expression, the mixtures of community and privacy, fond familiarity and quick change and escape, which this minuscule subdivision and diversification of the quarter-acre's spaces can offer to the lives it houses. Compared with it, the private realm of the city apartment is internally monotonous, and its owner more restricted in what he can make of it. He loses a whole field for self-expression, and many chances to adapt his environment to idiosyncratic needs. He has only one escape. That one may be into the crowded city's full and valuable diversity, but he can't go there undressed. The escape is to nowhere quiet or private, to nothing he can kick, dig up, re-plan, encourage to grow, or hang a wet shirt on. In many cities the landless city apartment is where the rich get most neuroses and the poor get most delinquents.

Above all the house-in-garden is the most freely and cheaply flexible of all housing forms. Tents are its only competitors. It can be altered and extended in more ways and directions, with less hindrance from laws or neighbours, to meet more changes of need, than any denser housing can be. Each owner has considerable freedom to choose his own degree of privacy, publicity or neighbourliness. This freedom to alter his house without changing his address is an underrated one.

Many people like gardens, and gardening. Nobody knows, but I guess that those who do what they like with their gardens, and like doing it, probably outnumber the reluctant conformists. And many more things than gardening go on behind those fences – there's no need to catalogue the hobbies and small trades and storages, all the arts and crafts and mercifully private disasters that clutter people's back yards. Children's uses of them are probably the most valuable of all – and not only to the children. Home allows the widest variety of outdoor activities and constructions, especially the complicated, continuing, accumulating ones. The players can build their own scenery and sets, and keep them intact for serials. Collectors can house their zoos. Parents, children, visitors, and the relations between them, all share in the benefits. In some urban circumstances (or social classes) children can't 'go out' without due notice, a change of clothes, and a minder. But private suburban gardens let them mind their own business, much of which (like writing some of this chapter) is consistent with keeping an intermittent eye or ear on children moving freely about the resources of their own and neighbouring children's houses and gardens.

So – to sum up – you don't have to be a mindless conformist to choose suburban life. Most of the best poets and painters and inventors and protesters choose it too.

7

Empty and Flat

The emptiness and flatness of the country have been regarded by some as a fitting symbol of Australians and their society. Australia is seen as a society not well rooted in its place, with the people inexpressive and not closely engaged with each other. But the emptiness also gives hope that something fresh may emerge from the desert.

LIKE THE SUBURBS OF LONDON

Beatrice and Sidney Webb were husband and wife who operated as a formidable research and writing team for progressive causes in Britain. They visited Australia in 1898. They were impressed with the efficiency and honesty of Australian democratic government; Beatrice was not impressed by the tone of colonial society.

How can we begin about Australia? 'Too great and ambitious for affection, and yet not great enough for respect.' (Charles Darwin) Neither in its country nor in its people has it the charm of New Zealand. Plain, mountain, undulating hill and dale, all alike covered with the monotonous Eucalyptus; glaring sun, everlasting winds carrying clouds of dust, dry nervous air, sickly colouring, the consciousness of the unreclaimable waste of the interior on the one hand, and of the interminable ocean on the other, gives to life in Australia a desolate combination of restlessness and ennui unknown in beautiful, fertile and wonderfully varied New Zealand. As for society in Australia, it is just a slice of Great Britain and differs only slightly from Glasgow, Manchester, Liverpool and the *suburbs* of London. Bad manners, ugly clothes, vigour and shrewdness characterise the settlements of Sydney, Melbourne and of bush stations, exactly as they characterise the lower and upper middle class folk of the old country. If anything the manners are worse, the dress more pretentious and glaring and lacking in taste, than with us! The well-to-do women especially lack culture, charm and any kind of grace; and the richer they are the more objectionable they become.

NO SOUL

D.H. Lawrence was a controversial English novelist. He explored what was deep and hidden in relations between people, which meant he discussed sexual relations much more explicitly than previously. He visited Australia briefly in 1922 and was alternately attracted and repulsed by it. He expressed his views in the novel Kangaroo (in which the character Somers is the mouthpiece for Lawrence himself; Harriet is his wife) and in letters to friends.

They went home in a motor-bus and a cloud of dust, with the heaven bluer than blue above, the hills dark and fascinating, and the land so remote-seeming. Everything so clear, so very distinct, and yet so marvellously aloof.

And the occupants of the bus bouncing and bobbing like a circus, because of the very bumpy road.

'Shakes your dinner down,' said the old woman with the terribly home-made hat – oh, such difficult, awful hats.

'It does, if you've had any,' laughed Harriet.

'Why, you've 'ad your dinner, 'aven't you?'

As concerned as if Harriet was her own stomach, such a nice old woman. And a lovely little boy with the bright, wide, gentle eyes of these Australians. So alert and alive and with that lovableness that almost hurts one. Absolute trust in the 'niceness' of the world. A tall, stalky, ginger man with the same bright eyes and a turned-up nose and long stalky legs. An elderly man with bright, friendly, elderly eyes and careless hair and careless clothing. He was Joe, and the other was Alf. Real careless Australians, careless of their appearance, careless of their speech, of their money, of everything – except of their happy-go-lucky democratic friendliness. Really nice, with bright, quick, willing eyes. The driver's face was long and deep red. He was absolutely laconic. And yet, absolutely willing, as if life held no other possibility than that of being an absolutely willing citizen. A fat man with a fat little girl waiting at one of the corners.

'Up she goes!' he said as he lifted her in.

A perpetual, unchanging willingness, and an absolute equality. The same good-humoured, right-you-are approach from everybody to everybody. 'Right-you are! Right-O' Somers had been told so many hundreds of times, Right-he-was, Right-O, that he almost dropped into the way of it. It was like sleeping between blankets – so cosy. So cosy.

So nice, so nice, so gentle. The strange, bright-eyed gentleness. Of course really rub him the wrong way, and you've got a Tartar. But not before you've asked for one. Gentle as a Kangaroo or a wallaby, with that wide-eyed, bright-eyed alert, *responsible* gentleness Somers had never known in Europe. It had a great beauty. And at the same time it made his spirits sink.

...

If you want to know what it is to feel the 'correct' social world fizzle to nothing, you should come to Australia. It *is* a weird place. In the *established* sense, it is socially nil. Happy-go-lucky, don't-you-bother, we're-in-Australia. But also there seems to be no inside life of any sort: just a long lapse and drift. A rather fascinating indifference, a *physical* indifference to what we call soul or spirit. It's really a weird show. The country has an extraordinary hoary, weird attraction. As you get used to it, it seems so *old*, as if it had missed all this Semite-Egyptian-Indo-European vast era of history, and was coal age, the age of great ferns and mosses. It hasn't got a consciousness – just none – too far back. A strange effect it has on one. Often I hate it like poison, then again it fascinates me, and the spell of its indifference gets me. I can't quite explain it: as if one resolved back almost to the plant kingdom, before souls, spirits and minds were grown at all: only quite a live, energetic body with a weird face.

NO TRADITION

The 1935 newspaper article on 'The Future of Australian literature' by G.H. Cowling, the English-born Professor of Literature at Melbourne University, prompted a furious response from those writers who were hoping to create a rich and distinctive Australian literature.

In spite of what the native-born say about gum trees, I cannot help feeling that our countryside is 'thin' and lacking in tradition. Do not misunderstand me; I am not criticising Australia. I love the country. I admire its beauty. I take off my hat to the countryman and his splendid mate the country woman. What I mean is there are no ancient churches, castles, ruins – the memorials of generations departed. Australia lacks the richness of age and tradition. This being so we are driven to invent a conventional field of a very limited extent, including 'the old station', 'the old mine', 'the old family' and 'the young opera singer'. These conventional themes are lacking in vitality. Their variations are exhausted. We want fresh themes. We need new paths. Romance always languishing has died. Realism without a striking personality behind it is not enough.

Poetry at the moment is out of fashion. But biography, travel, popular science and the novel are distinctly in demand. What scope is there for Australian biography? Little, I should say. There are few good subjects from the limited character of the country. I could name perhaps six good ones, but few of them possess the interest and 'colour' of European biographies. What scope is there for books on travel? Little I think. Australian travel is too sameish. On the other hand, there should be great scope for Australian books of popular science, and I am surprised that more is not done in this field.

Lastly we come to the novel. The novel should attract great writers, because it is now definitely a trade. Novel writing means supplying the libraries with seven and sixpenny fiction. There are exceptions of course but Australia is not the place in which to be a James Joyce. I think there are distinct possibilities here if we can remember that literary culture is not indigenous, like the gum tree, but is from a European source. Good Australian novels, which are entirely Australian, are bound to be few.

WILL PROPHETS COME FROM THE DESERT?

The Jindyworobak movement, formed in 1938, hoped that by working from the Australian landscape and Aboriginal culture a distinctively Australian literature could be created. The poet A.D. Hope was far from being a Jindyworobak; he believed with Professor Cowling that literature in Australia had to grow out of the European tradition. But in his 'Australia' (1939) he gave some hope for a distinctively Australian voice.

A Nation of trees, drab green and desolate grey
In the field uniform of modern wars,
Darkens her hills, those endless, outstretched paws
Of Sphinx demolished or stone lion worn away.

They call her a young country, but they lie:
She is the last of lands, the emptiest,
A woman beyond her change of life, a breast
Still tender but within the womb is dry.

Without songs, architecture, history:
The emotions and superstitions of younger lands,
Her rivers of water drown among inland sands,
The river of her immense stupidity

Floods her monotonous tribes from Cairns to Perth.
In them at last the ultimate men arrive
Whose boast is not: 'we live' but 'we survive',
A type who will inhabit the dying earth.

And her five cities, like five teeming sores,
Each drains her: a vast parasite robber-state
Where second-hand Europeans pullulate
Timidly on the edge of alien shores.

Yet there are some like me turn gladly home
From the lush jungle of modern thought, to find
The Arabian desert of the human mind,
Hoping, if still from the deserts the prophets come,

Such savage and scarlet as no green hills dare
Springs in that waste, some spirit which escapes

The learned doubt, the chatter of cultured apes
Which is called civilization over there.

THE DESERT AND THE INFINITE

In 1973 Patrick White won the Nobel Prize for literature. His best-known novel is Voss (1957), which is loosely based on the explorations of the German explorer Ludwig Leichhardt. White too was exploring the 'desert' of Australia; he had returned after a long period in London and felt an outsider as a gay man and a highly cultivated writer.

'Can you tell me,' Le Mesurier had asked as they were standing on the white planks of the same ship, 'if you are coming to this damned country for any particular purpose?'

'Yes,' answered Voss, without hesitation. 'I will cross the continent from one end to the other. I have every intention to know it with my heart. Why I am pursued by this necessity, it is no more possible for me to tell than it is for you, who have made my acquaintance only before yesterday.'

They continued to look at the enormous sea.

'And what, may I ask in return, is your purpose? Mr Le Mesurier, is it?'

Some sense of kinship with the young man had made the German's accent kind.

'Purpose? So far, no purpose,' Le Mesurier said. 'But time will show, perhaps.'

It was clear that the vast glass of ocean would not.

…

Voss had encountered Le Mesurier one evening at dusk amongst the scrub and rocks gathered together above the water on the northern side of the Domain, and asked, as it seemed the time and place:

'Have you discovered that purpose, Frank, that we have discussed already on board the ship?'

'Why no, I have not, Mr Voss,' said the elusive Frank, and the goose-flesh overcame him.

He began to pitch stones.

'I rather suspect,' he added, 'it is something I shall not discover till I am at my last gasp.'

Then Voss, who had sat down in a clearing in the scrub and larger, ragged trees, warmed more than ever to the young man, knowing what it was to wrestle with his own daemon. In the darkening, yellow light, the German's arms around his knees were spare as willow switches. He could dispense with flesh.

Le Mesurier continued to throw stones, that made a savage sound upon the rocks.

Then Voss had said:

'I have a proposition to make. My plans are forming. It is intended that I will lead an expedition into the interior, westward from the Darling Downs. Several gentlemen of this town are interested in the undertaking, and will provide me with the necessary backing. Do you care to come, Frank?'

'I?' exclaimed Le Mesurier.

And he pitched a particularly savage stone.

'No,' he said, lingeringly. 'I am not sure that I want to cut my throat just yet.'

'To make yourself, it is also necessary to destroy yourself,' said Voss.

He knew this young man as he knew his own blacker thoughts.

'I am aware of that,' laughed Frank. 'But I can do it in Sydney a damn sight more comfortably. You see, sir,' he added longingly, 'I am not intended for such heights as you. I shall wallow a little in the gutter, I expect, look at the stars from a distance, then turn over.'

'And your genius?' said the German.

'What genius?' asked Le Mesurier, and let fall the last of his ammunition.

'That remains to be seen. Every man has a genius, though it is not always discoverable. Least of all when choked by the trivialities of daily existence. But in this disturbing country, so far as I have become acquainted with it already, it is possible more easily to discard the inessential and to attempt the infinite. You will be burnt up most likely, you will have the flesh torn from your bones, you will be tortured in many horrible and primitive ways, but you will realize that genius of which you sometimes suspect you are possessed, and of which you will not tell me you are afraid.'

It was dark now. Tempted, the young man was, in fact, more than a little afraid – his throbbing body was deafening him – but as he was a vain young man, he was also flattered.

'That is so much, well, just so much,' protested Le Mesurier. 'You *are* mad,' he said.

'If you like,' said Voss.

NO NEED TO ASK QUESTIONS

The beach rather than the bush is where most Australians spend their leisure time. Donald Horne in The Lucky Country (1964) *gives a sympathetic account of Australian hedonism, as seen at the beach.*

Despite the puritanism that seeped into Australia through the Protestant sects, the Evangelical wing of the Church of England, the Irish Catholic Church, the Protestant Ethic (for businessmen) and the Nonconformist Conscience (for political leftwingers) there has been a counter-balancing paganism among ordinary people. When the waves are running right and the weather is fine the crowds at the beaches are doing more than enjoying themselves: they are worshipping the body and feeling identity with sand and sea and sky. Breaking through the disciplines of organized sport, people amuse themselves as they wish in outdoor games or relaxations that express a belief in the goodness of activity and nature. There has long been this element in Australia of delighting in life for its vigour and activity, without asking questions about it. It has received considerable literary expression as an unquestioning (and anti-intellectual as well as anti-puritan) hedonism, often with implied nature worship. It may be the philosophy of living of the young. When young men strap their malibu surf boards (cost £35 to £45) to their cars, drive off to the beach and command the breakers all day they seem to move into a life that is more Polynesian than puritan. In *Quadrant* Hugh Atkinson quoted a 'Surfie' as saying: 'I dunno, it's hard to describe. When you're driving hard and fast down the wall, with the soup curling behind yer, or doing this backside turn on a big one about to tube, it's just this feeling. Yer know, it leaves yer feeling stoked.'

It might be relevant to look at the life of the South Seas to throw some illumination on life in Australia, instead of the almost exclusive comparison with the United Kingdom and parts of Western Europe (ignoring Mediterranean Europe) with an occasional glance at the U.S.A. Desmond O'Grady wrote in the *Observer* of the sense of deprivation suffered by European migrants. 'They feel they are living in a void because the suburb has no organic relationship to the city. Those Italians who are disappointed because they feel that they do not belong, that they have not reached the centre of Australian life will go on feeling disappointed because there is no centre. Once they realize there is no centre and they couldn't care less about it, they'll have been assimilated.' Yet the place to send migrants so that they can feel they belong is to the beach, one of the strongest centres of gregariousness in the ocean cities. Australians do not sit at pavement cafes to watch the promenade. They go to the beach, sun themselves and surf, and watch the promenade there. They still look at people, but the people have most of their clothes off. Here a young man can show his prowess in the water to his peers and the women of his tribe, his existence stripped down to what he alone feels and sees (which isn't much); his father may be in the men's quarters telling stories of war, of fishing, or of sporting ritual; others may be sailing or looking to the garden. There is also in Australian life some of the craving for quietness and slow reflection. A man likes to sit in the sun and say nothing, do nothing and think very little. On holidays Australians like to retreat to shacks or even tents beside the water, and enjoy the primitive.

ANYONE CAN FEEL AT HOME

The experimental writer Anna Couani is of Greek Australian descent. In Were all the women sex-mad? *(1982), a novella in dialogue, she renders the views of an Englishman who is a tourist in Europe and who has previously visited Australia. This speech echoes Lawrence's criticisms – and suggests why Australia is an easy society to fit into.*

Night after night after night in the bars of Amsterdam we talked about the ways different countries differed.

– You know I've travelled all over the world don't you – any place you can name. Well, I'll tell you this – Australia's great for a holiday but I wouldn't live there. It's unique I'll say that. Anyone can feel at home there because it has a strange character or atmosphere that is like an absence of character, a kind of neutrality. I think it's very tolerant or maybe just very anonymous. No really, I do *like* Australia. When I lived there I liked it. But I realize coming away again that there's some strange pressure there. It's subliminal, very subtle. I don't think I could describe it exactly because it's an abstract quality that pervades everything there, the work situation, the politics, the social life. It's a place that gets you down. The amount of drinking the people do is phenomenal. And it's as though everyone's bitten by the same bug – some kind of desperation or hysteria that is never expressed. They're stoics, the Aussies. The most cynical people in the world. Beyond morality – like the English but more sophisticated because they never say *anything*. The English talk and talk and talk, endlessly trying to reason things out, playing with words really but they're expressing attitudes. The *real* Australian attitude is never expressed. If you talk to an Australian about being Australian, they just say, 'What's it to you', or 'Why don't you go back to Ponseville, mate, where you belong', or 'Want a match? Your face and my arse. Christ all this talking's given me a thirst'. They're always on the defensive. To get an opinion out of them is like getting blood from a stone. They think conversation on a serious level is a joke. Not that they're so wrong. I'm sure they know they have opinions and that you might differ in opinion but that seems irrelevant to them. They just laugh and say, 'Don't get your tits in a tangle, come and have a beer.' They make friends with the people they happen to be thrown together with, not necessarily the people they like.

8

Put-downs

All these criticisms – direct or implied – were made by people who did not live here, except the last. The Australian character has been formed in part in reaction to the put-downs of outsiders, especially the English. The alternative to rejecting the criticisms was to embrace them, an attitude that was dubbed 'the cultural cringe' by A.A. Phillips, a leading man of letters in the 1950s and 1960s. The last extract is a fine example of the cringe.

∾ CHARLES DARWIN, *English naturalist who visited in 1836.*
The whole population, poor and rich, are bent on acquiring wealth: amongst the highest orders, wool and sheep-grazing form the constant subject of conversation.

A Naturalist's Voyage (1879), p. 444

∾ Anon (1850s).
There vice is virtue, virtue vice,
And all that's vile is voted nice

F.G. Clarke, *The Land of Contrarieties* (1977), p. 170

∾ CHARLES DICKENS, *English novelist.*
In David Copperfield Dickens ships off a number of his characters to Australia, among them Emily, Mr Peggotty's daughter, who has been 'ruined' by running away with the cad Steerforth.

'You have quite made up your mind,' said I to Mr. Peggotty, 'as to the future, good friend? I need scarcely ask you.'

'Quite, Mas'r Davy,' he returned; 'and told Em'ly. Theer's mighty countries fur from here. Our future life lays over the sea.'

'They will emigrate together, aunt,' said I.

'Yes!' said Mr. Peggotty, with a hopeful smile. 'No-one can't reproach my darling in Australia. We will begin a new life over there!'

David Copperfield (1850), ch. 51

∾ English cricketer, when spectators invaded the Sydney Cricket Ground in 1879.

You sons of convicts.

Sydney Morning Herald, 10 February 1879

∾ ANTHONY TROLLOPE, English novelist who visited in 1871–72. The wonders performed in the way of riding, driving, fighting, walking, working, drinking, love-making, and speech-making, which men and women in Australia told me of themselves, would have been worth recording in a separate volume had they been related by any but the heroes and heroines themselves. But reaching one as they do always in the first person, these stories are soon received as works of a fine art much cultivated in the colonies, for which the colonial phrase of 'blowing' has been created. When a gentleman sounds his own trumpet he 'blows'. The art is perfectly understood and appreciated among the people who practise it. Such a gentleman or such a lady was only 'blowing'! You hear it and hear of it every day. They blow a good deal in Queensland; – a good deal in South Australia. They blow even in poor Tasmania. They blow loudly in New South Wales, and very loudly in New Zealand. But the blast of the trumpet as heard in Victoria is louder than all the blasts, – and the Melbourne blast beats all the other blowing of that proud colony. My first, my constant, my parting advice to my Australian cousins is contained in two words – 'Don't blow.'

Australia (1967), pp. 375–6

❧ J.A. FROUDE, *English historian who visited in 1885.*
It is hard to quarrel with men who only wish to be innocently happy.

Oceana (1886), p. 191

❧ OSCAR WILDE, *Irish playwright.*
CECILY: I think you had better wait till Uncle Jack arrives. I know he wants to speak to you about your emigrating.

ALGERNON: About my what?

CECILY: Your emigrating. He has gone up to buy your outfit.

ALGERNON: I certainly wouldn't let Jack buy my outfit. He has no taste in neckties at all.

CECILY: I don't think you will require neckties. Uncle Jack is sending you to Australia.

ALGERNON: Australia! I'd sooner die.

The Importance of Being Earnest (1895), Act II

❧ D.H. LAWRENCE, *English novelist who visited in 1922.*
This is the most democratic place I have ever been in. And the more I see of democracy the more I dislike it. It just brings everything down to the mere vulgar level of wages and prices, electric light and water closets, and nothing else.

The Collected Letters of D.H. Lawrence, vol. 4, p. 263

❧ H.G. WELLS, *English novelist who visited in 1938–39.*
Australia, very much Americanised, but intensely British, is not
yet a nation.

Age, 27 January 1939

❧ WINSTON CHURCHILL, *British Prime Minister in World War II.*
The P.M. is in a belligerent mood. He told us that he had sent a stiff
telegram, to Curtin, the Prime Minister of Australia. The situation
in Malaya was making Australia jumpy about invasion. Curtin
was not satisfied with the air position. He had renewed his repre-
sentations to London in blunt terms. The P.M. fulminated in his
reply. London had not made a fuss when it was bombed. Why
should Australia? At one moment he took the line that Curtin and
his Government did not represent the people of Australia. At
another that the Australians came of bad stock. He was impatient
with people who had nothing better to do than criticise him.

Lord Moran, *Winston Churchill* (1966), p. 21

❧ US *General* DOUGLAS MACARTHUR, *on the Australians fighting
on the Kokoda Track, 1942.*
Operations reports show that progress on the trail is NOT repeat
NOT satisfactory.

To which Major General A.S. Allen drafted this reply: 'If you
think you can do any better come up and bloody try' (which he did
not send).

David Horner, *Crisis of Command* (1978), pp. 209–10

❧ GERMAINE GREER, *Australian feminist resident in England.*
Australia is a huge rest home, where no unwelcome news is ever
wafted on to the pages of the worst newspapers in the world.

London Observer, 1 August 1982

∾ PAUL KEATING, *Australian Prime Minister 1991–96.*
Patrick White and I never had a lot in common but one thing we certainly had in common – he said 'sport has addled the Australian consciousness' and I think it has.

Age, 17 November 2005

We'll be off to Europe. We won't be staying here – this is the arse-end of the earth.

Bob Hawke, *Memoirs* (1994), p. 501

9

Sport

In Europe villages grew up around churches. In Australia when a stopping place became a settlement, it acquired first a pub and then a race-track – so complained the Rev. J.D. Lang, the pioneer Presbyterian clergyman. Horse-racing was the colonists' first sport, a natural consequence of so many men using horses for their work. From the second half of the nineteenth century organised team sports flourished, along with complaints that Australians gave too much attention to them.

THE RACING CALENDAR

An early Sydney judge said the court should supply him with a racing calendar since so many witnesses dated events according to the winners of notable races. The Catholic priest cum poet 'John O'Brien' dealt with the phenomenon in 'Tangmalangaloo' in his collection Around the Boree Log (1921).

> The bishop sat in lordly state and purple cap sublime,
> And galvanized the old bush church at Confirmation time;
> And all the kids were mustered up from fifty miles around,
> With Sunday clothes, and staring eyes, and ignorance
>   profound.
> Now was it fate, or was it grace, whereby they yarded too
> An overgrown two-storey lad from Tangmalangaloo?

'Come, tell me, boy,' his lordship said in crushing tones severe,
'Come, tell me why is Christmas Day the greatest of the year?
'How is it that around the world we celebrate that day
'And send a name upon a card to those who're far away?
'Why is it wandering ones return with smiles and greetings,
    too?'
A squall of knowledge hit the lad from Tangmalangaloo.

He gave a lurch which set a-shake the vases on the shelf,
He knocked the benches all askew, up-ending of himself.
And oh, how pleased his lordship was, and how he smiled
    to say,
'That's good, my boy. Come, tell me now; and what is
    Christmas Day?'
The ready answer bared a fact no bishop ever knew –
'It's the day before the races out at Tangmalangaloo.'

THE MOST SPORTING COUNTRY IN THE WORLD

Richard Twopeny in Town Life in Australia *(1883) explains the attachment to sport. He was writing just after Australia first won the 'Ashes' in a cricket test against England.*

The abundance of fine and temperate weather makes outdoor life preferable to indoor during eight months of the year. Perhaps this is a reason why the colonists live in such poor houses and care so little how they are furnished. Town-life is a recent invention in Australia; and town-life as it is known at home, in the sense that numbers of people live in a town all their lives and only go into the country for an airing, is quite unknown. The majority of the population still lives, more or less, in the bush. Our ideals are country ideals and not town ideals. For all these reasons the principal amusements of the Australian are outdoor sports of one kind or another; and if the interest taken in them proportionate to the population be the criterion, this may fairly claim to be the most sporting country in the world. In Australia alone, of all countries, can any sport be called national in the sense that the whole nation from the oldest greybeard to the youngest child, takes an interest in it.

Cricket must, I suppose, take the first place amongst Australian sports, because all ages and all classes are interested in it; and not to be interested in it amounts almost to a social crime. The quality of Australian cricket has already spoken for itself in England. Of its quantity it is difficult to give any idea. Cricket clubs are perhaps numerable, though yearly increasing; but of the game itself there is no end. There is no class too poor to play, as at home. Every little Australian that is 'born alive' is a little cricketer, a bat, or bowler, or field. Cricket is the colonial *carrière ouverte aux talents*. As Napoleon's soldiers remembered that they carried a marshal's *baton* in their knapsacks, so the young Australians all remember that they have a chance of becoming successors of that illustrious band of heroes who have recently conquered the mother-country and looted her into the bargain, though the idea of gain certainly never enters into their heads in connection with cricket. It may be, and it is most probable, that English cricket will soon recover the laurels which the Australian carried away in 1882; but I venture to prophesy that from 1890 onwards, the cricket championship will, except through occasional bad-luck, become permanently resident in Australia. The success of the first Australian Eleven bred cricketers by the thousand. If that eleven was picked out of, say, 10,000 men and boys playing cricket, the present has been chosen from 20,000, and by 1890 the eleven will be chosen from 100,000.

*

THE NATIONAL DAY

The American novelist Mark Twain visited in 1895 and in Following the Equator (1897) he records his surprise at the significance of a horse-race.

It is the mitred Metropolitan of the Horse-Racing Cult. Its race-ground is the Mecca of Australasia. On the great annual day of sacrifice – the 5th of November, Guy Fawkes's Day – business is suspended over a stretch of land and sea as wide as from New York to San Francisco, and deeper than from the northern lakes to the Gulf of Mexico; and every man and woman, of high degree or low, who can afford the expense, put away their other duties and come. They begin to swarm in by ship and rail a fortnight before the day, and they swarm thicker and thicker day after day, until all the vehicles of transportation are taxed to their uttermost to meet the demands of the occasion, and all hotels and lodgings are bulging outward because of the pressure from within. They come a hundred thousand strong, as all the best authorities say, and they pack the spacious grounds and grand-stands and make a spectacle such as is never to be seen in Australasia elsewhere.

It is the 'Melbourne Cup' that brings this multitude together. Their clothes have been ordered long ago, at unlimited cost, and without bounds as to beauty and magnificence, and they have been kept in concealment until now, for unto this day are they consecrate. I am speaking of the *ladies'* clothes; but one might know that.

And so the grand-stands make a brilliant and wonderful spectacle, a delirium of color, a vision of beauty. The champagne flows, everybody is vivacious, excited, happy; everybody bets, and gloves and fortunes change hands right along, all the time. Day after day the races go on, and the fun and the excitement are kept at white heat; and when each day is done, the people dance all night so as to be fresh for the race in the morning. And at the end of the great week the swarms secure lodgings and transportation for next year, then flock away to their remote homes and count their gains and losses, and order next year's Cup-clothes, and then lie down and sleep two weeks, and get up sorry to reflect that a whole year must be put in somehow or other before they can be wholly happy again.

The Melbourne Cup is the Australasian National Day. It would be difficult to overstate its importance. It overshadows all other holidays and specialized days of whatever sort in that congeries of colonies. Overshadows them? I might almost say it blots them out. Each of them gets attention, but not everybody's; each of them evokes interest, but not everybody's; each of them rouses enthusiasm, but not everybody's; in each case a part of the attention, interest, and enthusiasm is a matter of habit and custom, and another part of it is official and perfunctory. Cup Day, and Cup Day only, commands an attention, an interest, and an enthusiasm which are universal – and spontaneous, not perfunctory. Cup Day is supreme – it has no rival. I can call to mind no specialized annual day, in any country, which can be named by that large name – Supreme. I can call to mind no specialized annual day, in any country, whose approach fires the whole land with a conflagration of conversation and preparation and anticipation and jubilation. No day save this one; but this one does it.

ONLY SPORT MATTERS

The Daily Telegraph (Melbourne), 27 February 1883, carried one of many condemnations of Young Australia's interest in sport.

There is one marked characteristic in the disposition of the typical young Australian, which bodes unfavourably for his further intellectual and moral development. We refer, of course, to his inordinate addiction to athletic sports and pastimes. He is nothing if not a cricketer, a footballer, or a rowing man. To handle a bat deftly, to be able to kick an inflated bladder to a greater distance than any other fellow, or to handle an oar with skill and dexterity, appears to be the very climax of his ambition. Then he is in his element, and feels himself to be somebody, and boldly challenges the admiration of all the world for the great athletic champion. Of this he talks by day, and dreams by night. It is more to him than his daily business, his moral duties, his mental advancement, all combined.

The fall of a wicket takes precedence, in his estimation, of the fall of a kingdom. What cares he for the people on the other side of the globe? Of what concern is it to him that the great empire in which he enjoys the proud privilege of citizenship, is perturbed to her very centre? What does he know or care about France or Germany, Russia or Austria, the revolt in the Danubian principalities, or the condition of India, China, Japan? Talk to him of the tremendous score that Murdoch made the other day, or the mighty feats of the 'Demon Bowler', and you draw from him all the interest and the deep feeling of which his nature is capable.

This over-mastering passion for athletic sports is showing its power even in public life. The younger generation now possesses the privilege of the franchise. And of what class is the typical young Australian candidate? Naturally of the same class as his ardent admirers and supporters. In other words, he is, simply, a cricketer, or a footballer, or a rowing man, or some form of athlete. To be captain of the team is to be the very man to make laws for and govern the country.

AN ANGLO-SAXON INVENTION

The defenders of the young Australians' interest in sport posed the question: from whom did they learn the love of sport? The British were a sporting nation and ran a sporting empire, which has had its effect on Australia, as David Malouf explores in Made in England (2003).

Sport as we understand it was an Anglo-Saxon invention of the late eighteenth and early nineteenth century. The English made it central, both as a physical activity and as moral training, to their whole system of education. Wellington's famous dictum, that the battle of Waterloo was won on the playing fields of Eton, must have been as incomprehensible to his Prussian and Russian allies as it was to the French, but has endured as a kind of shorthand for a culture in which the playing field, like the Greek palestra, is seen as a training ground for life; for the development of Athenian minds in Spartan bodies, and for an ethos in which terms like 'fair play', 'sportsmanship', 'team spirit' are meant to be translated out of the narrow world of schoolboy rivalry and endeavour into the world of action and affairs; not as metaphors but as practical forms of behaviour.

The supply of dedicated civil servants and subalterns who ran the Empire, especially India, depended on this ethos and on the education system that sustained it. Nowhere but in the Anglo-Saxon world, and in places like India, Pakistan and parts of Asia, Africa and the Pacific where English forms of education have been 'naturalised' – along with school uniforms, the prefect system, sports halfs, houses – has organised sport become an integral part of the school curriculum, the central place where that discipline of the spirit as well as the body is developed that is at the very centre of the culture.

Can we imagine how much thinner our involvement with the

rest of the world might be if this peculiar Anglo-Saxon passion had not worked on us, and on the Pakistanis and Indians, and the West Indians, New Zealanders, South Africans and others, who come together to play one-day and Test cricket and Rugby Union and League football? It has made alliances for us with peoples with whom we have a special relationship in which we are trusted to 'play fair', and to speak fair too, that has been extended, at times, into other areas where we are also trusted – as in our stand on Apartheid in the '70s and '80s, in Fiji during the crisis of the '90s, and in the Solomons now. It was the teams we sent to England in the 1870s that first established us, in British eyes, as a single nation, long before we had made the move to official nationhood, and it was through rivalry on the field, in which we often turned out to be superior, that a kind of equality grew up between us when in other areas the Australian states were still minor dependents. The symbol of the Ashes, playful as it was, gave Australia a place in British popular mythology that none of the other colonies enjoyed, and in an area that mattered, had weight, in a way that, outside the magic circle of Anglo-Saxon thinking, would have been incomprehensible. It is small things that make up the real fabric of a relationship; things that 'history' may not know about or miss. But then sport is just the sort of area where to make too much of a thing would be to miss the real thing altogether.

A REVOLT AGAINST ENGLAND

The most ferocious official attack on England ever coming out of Australia occurred in the realm of sport. In 1933 the Australian Cricket Board accused English test cricketers of being 'unsportsmanlike'. This was in response to the use of 'bodyline' bowling by Larwood at the instigation of his captain, Jardine. The English authorities refused to believe the charge and were outraged at how the Australian crowds had reacted to 'bodyline' bowling, as Laurence Le Quesne explains in The Bodyline Controversy *(1983).*

Australian crowds were, by and large, noisier and more outspoken than English ones. This no doubt owed something to the fact that they tended to be bigger (since there was more accommodation for them); but there was more to it than that. The behaviour of English cricket crowds – at least of southern English ones – between the Wars was still bound by conventions so strict as to look in retrospect positively Victorian: traditionally, they applauded, and on occasion they cheered, but they did not shout, they did not criticize, and certainly they did not boo. The further from London, and especially the further north, you went, the less this was true. Yorkshire and Lancashire crowds had a longstanding reputation for apt and salty comment on incidents in the field. But even in the heat of the Roses matches, booing seems to have been unheard of; and in any case, it was Lord's rather than Headingley or Old Trafford that set the official standards of good behaviour.

In the less inhibited and more democratic society of Australia, they ordered things differently. Crowds there were accustomed to keeping up a running commentary on what went on before them, and to venting their sense of humour, and their approbation and disapprobation of individual players, with a freedom unheard of in England. Individual players reacted to this differently. Some never liked it – the stiffly correct Jardine is a classic example of this reaction: his experience of Australian crowds during the 1928 tour seems to have been a major source of his enduring antipathy to Australia and Australian behaviour – and these included some Australians: the Test all-rounder Alan Fairfax objected to it so strongly that he walked out of first-class cricket altogether. No doubt, according to a widely-recognized rule of human behaviour, those who showed their dislike of it got the worst of it as a result.

Others, those who took the crowd's ribaldry in good part and showed that they had a sense of humour themselves, found that the crowd too were equally capable of enjoying a joke at their own expense: 'Gawd, I could have caught that one with my mouth!'; 'So could I, if I had a mouth as big as yours' – that sort of thing went down well in the outfield. Similarly, not even Jardine minded when a flight of pigeons flew over the Oval at Adelaide during the third Test, and somebody shouted, 'Don't go away – there he is at mid-on.' But when it was a matter of a crowd expressing mass disapproval of the way one side was playing the game – of unduly slow batting, for example – obviously not much could be achieved by individual repartee.

In the great anti-'bodyline' demonstrations of 1933, this was the case in an extreme degree, and there is no question that such demonstrations could be unpleasant and on occasion frightening things. A crowd of 40,000 booing, hooting, catcalling, counting bowlers out, throwing orange peel (though never apparently anything more dangerous than that) at outfielders, and so on, is not a pleasant spectacle. But was this outrageous partisanship, or fair comment on one side's tactics?

Since the English newspaper reader had no notion that his bowlers were doing anything questionable, and since the conventions of crowd behaviour in the two countries were so different, it is not surprising if he soon came to see the real source of the trouble that was going on in Australia not as English bowling, but as Australian bad sportsmanship and bad manners – the conduct of what a *Times* correspondent summed up as 'larrikins, habitual loafers, deadbeats ... and irresponsible youths who will always follow the lead of rowdy seniors'. This did not conduce to a swift and friendly settlement of the dispute.

DREAM SYMBOL

Aborigines, excluded from white society, could succeed in sport, first in cricket, later in boxing and football. Since sportspeople are so admired, no higher honour could be given to an Australian than to light the torch at the Sydney Olympics in 2000. The Aboriginal middle-distance runner Cathy Freeman was chosen for this task. The BBC reported on its significance.

The so-called 'Friendly games' opened with a gesture of Australian national reconciliation when the country's star athlete, Cathy Freeman, was chosen to light the Olympic flame.

The 27-year-old national superstar is not only a favourite to win the 400 metres, she is also of Aboriginal descent – and a political figure who is outspoken in her defence of the rights of Australia's indigenous people.

The choice of her as the athlete to star at the climactic moment of the opening ceremony may be dismissed by critics as gesture politics. But it nevertheless may also be seen as carrying a resonance that goes beyond cynicism.

Freeman is a potent symbol of the way in which Australia would like to be perceived by the world – an open, multi-cultural and tolerant society – but also of the problems for which many, including Freeman, have criticised it in the past.

For many Aborigines, the Games represent an opportunity to expose their cause to the world at large.

It could be argued that the organising committee could hardly avoid celebrating Aboriginal culture. And it did so in a 'Deep Sea Dreaming' sequence in which Aboriginal dancers conjured a giant Wandjina, a spirit symbolising the unity of the indigenous people.

But in doing so, and choosing Freeman to light the flame, it sent an important signal that the country cannot hide from its past.

Six years ago, Freeman was rebuked by officials when she won the 400m at the Commonwealth games in Canada and took a victory lap carrying the Aboriginal flag.

That will not be a problem this year – the Australian Olympic Committee has said it will not punish athletes who celebrate with that flag.

That turnaround is no doubt due in no small part to Freeman, who has campaigned fearlessly in defence of the Aborigines.

There have been calls for an Aboriginal boycott of the Sydney Games, something which Freeman found herself under intense pressure to join – she only decided to run after the overwhelming majority of Aboriginal leaders said they supported her.

And as recently as July, she accused Australian leaders of insensitivity for refusing to apologise for government policies that forced the removal of 100,000 Aboriginal children from their homes from 1910 until the 1970s.

In that context, Freeman's march to the Olympic cauldron was a symbol of Australia's efforts to heal the wounds over the treatment of Aborigines.

She has come to personify that struggle, and as she jogged up the steps to light the flame, she received a roar that suggested she might well have been the people's choice.

IO

Anthems Official and Unofficial

Until the 1970s the Australian national anthem was 'God Save the Queen'. After a vote of the whole people it was replaced by 'Advance Australia Fair', which had been written by Peter McCormick in 1878. It has gradually gained acceptance but it is not as popular as other poems and songs that have become unofficial anthems.

ADVANCE AUSTRALIA FAIR

'Advance Australia' was a motto in use from the 1830s, over seventy years before there was a formal nation. Since Australia had a doubtful past and none of the glories of other nations, looking to the future was its only option. The song depicts Australia as having distinctive characteristics but the anxiety to identify it as British (a mixture of English, Scots and Irish) and to impress Britain is evident. The convict foundation is avoided. This is the original version taken from the 1879 sheet music held in the National Library. Of these verses only the first was adopted for the Anthem (with gender neutral language – 'Australians all'); the second verse of the Anthem comes from a later version of McCormick's song with some alterations.

> Australian sons, let us rejoice,
> For we are young and free;
> We've golden soil and wealth for toil,
> Our home is girt by sea;

Our land abounds in nature's gifts
Of beauty rich and rare;
In history's page, let every stage
Advance Australia Fair.

In joyful strains then let us sing
Advance Australia Fair.

When gallant Cook from Albion sailed,
To trace wide oceans o'er;
True British courage bore him on,
Til he landed on our shore;
Then here he raised Old England's flag,
The standard of the brave;
'With all her faults we love her still'
'Britannia rules the wave'.

In joyful strains then let us sing
Advance Australia Fair.

While other nations of the globe
Behold us from afar,
We'll rise to high renown and shine
Like our glorious southern star;
From English soil and Fatherland
Scotia and Erin fair,
Let all combine with heart and hand
To Advance Australia fair.

In joyful strains then let us sing
Advance Australia Fair.

Should foreign foe e'er sight our coast,
Or dare a foot to land,
We'll rouse to arms like sires of yore,
To guard our native strand;
Britannia then shall surely know
Though oceans roll between,
Her sons in fair Australia's land
Still keep their courage green.

In joyful strains then let us sing
Advance Australia Fair.

THE MAN FROM SNOWY RIVER

This poem by A.B. (Banjo) Paterson was first published in the Bulletin in 1890 and appeared in book form in The Man from Snowy River *and Other Verses in 1895, still the best-selling book of poetry published in Australia. The poem was not sung but thousands knew it by heart and recited it at concerts, pubs and around the camp fire. It celebrates a man's world where the only distinction between men is their capacity to ride horses.*

There was movement at the station, for the word had passed
    around
That the colt from old Regret had got away,
And had joined the wild bush horses – he was worth a thou-
    sand pound,
So all the cracks had gathered to the fray.
All the tried and noted riders from the stations near and far
Had mustered at the homestead overnight,

For the bushmen love hard riding where the wild bush horses
    are,
And the stock-horse snuffs the battle with delight.

There was Harrison, who made his pile when Pardon won the
    cup,
The old man with his hair as white as snow;
But few could ride beside him when his blood was fairly up –
He would go wherever horse and man could go.
And Clancy of the Overflow came down to lend a hand,
No better horseman ever held the reins;
For never horse could throw him while the saddle-girths
    would stand,
He learnt to ride while droving on the plains.

And one was there, a stripling on a small and weedy beast,
He was something like a racehorse undersized,
With a touch of Timor pony – three parts thoroughbred at
    least –
And such as are by mountain horsemen prized.
He was hard and tough and wiry – just the sort that won't say
    die –
There was courage in his quick impatient tread;
And he bore the badge of gameness in his bright and fiery eye,
And the proud and lofty carriage of his head.

But still so slight and weedy, one would doubt his power to
    stay,
And the old man said, 'That horse will never do
For a long and tiring gallop – lad, you'd better stop away,
Those hills are far too rough for such as you.'

So he waited sad and wistful – only Clancy stood his friend –
'I think we ought to let him come,' he said;
'I warrant he'll be with us when he's wanted at the end,
For both his horse and he are mountain bred.

'He hails from Snowy River, up by Kosciusko's side,
Where the hills are twice as steep and twice as rough,
Where a horse's hoofs strike firelight from the flint stones
    every stride,
The man that holds his own is good enough.
And the Snowy River riders on the mountains make their
    home,
Where the river runs those giant hills between;
I have seen full many horsemen since I first commenced to
    roam,
But nowhere yet such horsemen have I seen.'

So he went – they found the horses by the big mimosa clump –
They raced away towards the mountain's brow,
And the old man gave his orders, 'Boys, go at them from the
    jump,
No use to try for fancy riding now.
And, Clancy, you must wheel them, try and wheel them to the
    right.
Ride boldly, lad, and never fear the spills,
For never yet was rider that could keep the mob in sight,
If once they gain the shelter of those hills.'

So Clancy rode to wheel them – he was racing on the wing
Where the best and boldest riders take their place,
And he raced his stock-horse past them, and he made the
    ranges ring

With the stockwhip, as he met them face to face.
Then they halted for a moment, while he swung the dreaded
     lash,
But they saw their well-loved mountain full in view,
And they charged beneath the stockwhip with a sharp and
     sudden dash,
And off into the mountain scrub they flew.

Then fast the horsemen followed, where the gorges deep and
     black
Resounded to the thunder of their tread,
And the stockwhips woke the echoes, and they fiercely
     answered back
From cliffs and crags that beetled overhead.
And upward, ever upward, the wild horses held their way,
Where mountain ash and kurrajong grew wide;
And the old man muttered fiercely, 'We may bid the mob good
     day,
No man can hold them down the other side.'

When they reached the mountain's summit, even Clancy took
     a pull,
It well might make the boldest hold their breath,
The wild hop scrub grew thickly, and the hidden ground was
     full
Of wombat holes, and any slip was death.
But the man from Snowy River let the pony have his head,
And he swung his stockwhip round and gave a cheer,
And he raced him down the mountain like a torrent down its
     bed,
While the others stood and watched in very fear.

He sent the flint stones flying, but the pony kept his feet,
He cleared the fallen timber in his stride,
And the man from Snowy River never shifted in his seat –
It was grand to see that mountain horseman ride.
Through the stringy barks and saplings, on the rough and
    broken ground,
Down the hillside at a racing pace he went;
And he never drew the bridle till he landed safe and sound,
At the bottom of that terrible descent.

He was right among the horses as they climbed the further
    hill,
And the watchers on the mountain, standing mute,
Saw him ply the stockwhip fiercely, he was right among them
    still,
As he raced across the clearing in pursuit.
Then they lost him for a moment, where two mountain gullies
    met
In the ranges, but a final glimpse reveals
On a dim and distant hillside the wild horses racing yet,
With the man from Snowy River at their heels.

And he ran them single-handed till their sides were white
    with foam.
He followed like a bloodhound on their track,
Till they halted cowed and beaten, then he turned their heads
    for home,
And alone and unassisted brought them back.
But his hardy mountain pony he could scarcely raise a trot,
He was blood from hip to shoulder from the spur;
But his pluck was still undaunted, and his courage fiery hot,
For never yet was mountain horse a cur.

And down by Kosciusko, where the pine-clad ridges raise
Their torn and rugged battlements on high,
Where the air is clear as crystal, and the white stars fairly blaze
At midnight in the cold and frosty sky,
And where around the Overflow the reedbeds sweep and sway
To the breezes, and the rolling plains are wide,
The man from Snowy River is a household word to-day,
And the stockmen tell the story of his ride.

WALTZING MATILDA

'Waltzing Matilda' was included on the ballot that determined the national anthem and came second to 'Advance Australia Fair' partly because it was thought too informal for official status and perhaps because it was thought official status would spoil it. This rather than the official anthem is truly loved and is sung with real fervour. One of its attractions is that only Australians can understand it, though increasingly Australians too need a translation for many of its terms. Outsiders are puzzled that the story of a tramp or hobo can be embraced as a national symbol (the contrary impulse to wanting to impress the British, as in the original 'Advance Australia Fair'). The words were written in 1895 by Banjo Paterson while he was staying on a pastoral property in Queensland; the version commonly sung today, reproduced here, is slightly different. Just before his visit the pastoralists had defeated the shearers in a bitter strike. It has been suggested that the man who jumped into the billabong was wanted by the troopers for burning down the woolshed of the property where Paterson was staying.

Once a jolly swagman camped by a billabong
Under the shade of a coolibah tree
And he sang as he watched and waited 'til his billy boiled
'Who'll come a-waltzing Matilda with me?'

Waltzing Matilda, waltzing Matilda
Who'll come a-waltzing Matilda with me?
And he sang as he watched and waited 'til his billy boiled
'Who'll come a-waltzing Matilda with me?'

Along came a jumbuck to drink at that billabong
Up jumped the swagman and grabbed him with glee
And he sang as he shoved that jumbuck in his tucker bag
'You'll come a-waltzing Matilda with me'

Waltzing Matilda, waltzing Matilda
You'll come a-waltzing Matilda with me
And he sang as he shoved that jumbuck in his tucker bag
'You'll come a-waltzing Matilda with me'

Up rode the squatter mounted on his thoroughbred
Down came the troopers, one, two, three
'Where's that jolly jumbuck you've got in your tucker bag?'
You'll come a-waltzing Matilda with me

Waltzing Matilda, waltzing Matilda
You'll come a-waltzing Matilda with me
'Where's that jolly jumbuck you've got in your tucker bag?'
You'll come a-waltzing Matilda with me

Up jumped the swagman and sprang into that billabong
'You'll never take me alive,' said he
And his ghost may be heard as you pass by that billabong
'Who'll come a-waltzing Matilda with me?'

Waltzing Matilda, waltzing Matilda
Who'll come a-waltzing Matilda with me?

And his ghost may be heard as you pass by that billabong
'Who'll come a-waltzing Matilda with me?'

MY COUNTRY

*Dorothea Mackellar first published this poem with the title 'Core of My
Heart' in the London Spectator in 1908, and it is addressed to the English.
She called it 'My Country' when it appeared in a collection of her work in
1911 and by that title it was learnt by generations of schoolchildren. It is
the landmark statement of Australians' willingness to accept that they are
shaped by a landscape very different from England's. These are the first two
verses.*

The love of field and coppice,
Of green and shaded Lanes,
Of ordered woods and gardens,
Is running in your veins;
Strong love of grey-blue distance,
Brown streams and soft, dim skies –
I know but cannot share it,
My love is otherwise.

I love a sunburnt country,
A land of sweeping plains,
Of ragged mountain ranges,
Of drought and flooding rains,
I love her far horizons,
I love her jewel sea,
Her beauty and her terror –
The wide brown land for me.

THE AUSTRALAISE

This work of C.J. Dennis won the prize in a competition conducted in the Bulletin in 1908 for an Australian anthem. The word 'bloody' was to be inserted where there is a dash between words and (as in the last line of the chorus) within a word. Bloody was the commonest swear word, a crimson thread running through the language, as Joseph Furphy remarked in Such is Life, where he was highly inventive in conveying the talk that could not be rendered directly. Celebrating the crudities for which outsiders might look down on Australia is an ongoing national response, shared by those who might otherwise be cultivated. This is the first verse and the chorus.

> Fellers of Australier,
> Blokes an' coves an' coots,
> Shift yer — carcases,
> Move yer — boots.
> Gird yer — loins up,
> Get yer — gun,
> Set the — enermy
> An' watch the blighters run.
>
> Chorus
> Get a — move on,
> Have some — sense.
> Learn the — art of
> Self de- — -fence.

II

Surprises

Nations have a self-image which may not always relate closely to their true character. Here are some characteristics attributed to Australians, which are not part of the Australian self-image.

MUSICAL

Richard Twopeny in Town Life in Australia (1883).

Whether it is on account of the warmer climate I do not know, but certainly the colonists are a more musical people than the English. Of course I do not mean that there are any considerable number of people here who really understand classical music, or who play any instrument or sing really well. On the contrary, as I think I have said in some other connection, there is no part of the world where you hear so much bad music, professional and amateur. But it is also true, that there are few parts where you hear so much music. Almost every working-man has his girls taught to strum the piano. Amateur concerts are exceedingly popular. Most young people think they can sing, and Nature has certainly endowed the young colonials with, on the average, far better and more numerous voices than she has bestowed on English boys and girls. Sometimes when you are bored in a drawing-room by bad music and poor singing, you are inclined to think that the colonial love of music is an intolerable nuisance. Especially is this the case with me, who have been constantly interrupted in writing by my neighbour's daughters strumming the only two tunes they know – and those tunes 'Pinafore,' and 'Madame Angot.' But if you are out for a walk on a summer's evening, and look into the windows of working-men's cottages, you will see the old folk after their day's labour gathered round the piano in the sitting-room to hear their daughters play. I cannot hold with those who think a working-man's daughter should not learn music. Their reasoning is illogical – for being able to play the piano is in itself harmless, and may keep the girl out of mischief. Further, it gives a great deal of pleasure to her parents and friends, and often to herself as well.

*

The historian Geoffrey Blainey in Our Side of the Country (1984) considers why Australia produced good singers.

Nobody had any particular reason to expect that Victoria would produce famous singers, and yet it became even more famous overseas for its women singers than for its sportsmen. In recent decades Sydney has been more the home of acclaimed singers – Joan Hammond and Joan Sutherland both spent their childhood there – but Sydney for long had hardly a singer who sent ripples across the musical world, whereas the south-east corner of the continent – Hobart, Adelaide, and especially Victoria – produced a surprising number of singers who became famous in Europe.

Why Victoria, and Australia, should have produced such singers is not easily explained. A climate like that of Italy possibly helped. A widespread liking for music was a bonus, and many local organisations harnessed music to their sleigh. Nearly all the famous Victorian singers who emerged between the 1880s and the 1930s had performed when children with musical groups in churches, and some first made their name when they won a concert at eisteddfods, especially at the South Street competition in the cavernous wooden hall in Ballarat. It was not only a musical colony but a very competitive one, and music became one of the popular forms of competition. Opera to Australians of that era had some of the appeal of sport, and the critic Roger Covell has noted that opera has the same 'elements of sheer display and brazen dexterity'.

Singing became one of the few well-marked avenues to international fame for Australian girls. The public, by its own generous donations, was willing to send young Victorian singers along that avenue for a period of intensive training in opera in Europe, and they were prepared to marvel at the singers when they returned – a little fame seemed to improve the sound of the voice. To attend a concert given by a famous returning singer was one of the emotional landmarks in the life of thousands of Victorians. In effect an intricate superstructure of private support for promising singers had quietly arisen in Victoria, without any government lifting a finger or providing a penny. So often in Australia our success in producing champions came from an unplanned but hefty marshalling of resources which, in total, gave nearly as much stimulus as a nationalist government might provide today.

HONEST

Honesty was commonly mentioned by Turkish migrants talking of their experiences of Australians in The Turks in Australia *(1993).*

Vahide
Australians are very honest people. They are not preoccupied with cheating others like some nationalities. We worked in factories. They didn't try to discriminate against us or disadvantage us.

Melahat

In general I would describe Australians as a helpful and pleasant people. If you ask direction to somewhere they would go out of their way to show you. I haven't come across a bad Australian. I visited Germany once and the difference is stark. Germans are so mean to foreigners and not at all helpful or friendly. We went to a tea shop in Germany and asked for some tea. With a sour face they told us to serve ourselves. Here, people would politely assist you as much as they could. Once, though, I brought back a small present from Turkey for my supervisor in the factory. This is a customary gesture in our culture. He refused to accept it. I was so offended, I cried for days.

Niyazi

As far as I have dealings with them, Australians are an honest people. If we could speak better English we would never have any trouble with them. But once you 'um' and 'aahh' they think you are either a dill or are trying to cheese them off. They have no idea that you cannot put two words together in English.

Halim

Australians are good people, and most of them are educated. Ninety-nine per cent of them wouldn't lie. They have developed a good system of social rights. I like their laws and obey them.

PREJUDICED BUT NOT STUBBORN

Osvaldo Bonutto came to Queensland in the 1920s from Italy. He worked as timber-getter and canecutter before taking to running hotels. In A Migrant's Story (1994) he relates how he dealt with one customer in the hotel at Gordonvale near Cairns.

He started by calling me 'Mussolini', a nickname which I did not particularly cherish. I told him that if this was his idea of a joke, it was in very poor taste. If he persisted, I told him, the idea would be conveyed that I was a fascist which was anything but true. He was not so bad when he was sober but as soon as he got a bit tipsy, and that was pretty often, he was at it again, harping on politics, fascism and other irritating and contentious subjects with the sole object of provocation.

One evening he launched into the subject that Italians are not good settlers. I felt I had had enough of his bullying so I decided to give him a lecture. 'Listen, my friend,' I said, 'I have no more to do with Italian or international politics than you have. As far as migration and assimilation are concerned, this is neither the place nor the time to discuss them. Besides, these questions can only be discussed in a calm, unprejudiced frame of mind, which is not the case with you. By your open hostility towards me you have already proven that your mind is tainted with prejudice. I have come to Australia as a migrant to seek a new home. People like you are only retarding the process of assimilation, that gradual process of forgetting one's country and learning to love one's adopted country which you talk about but about which you know nothing.'

In the course of my harangue I found myself getting worked up and in order to prove my point concluded my speech by aiming a punch at him. He was standing in front of me across the bar and was quick enough to duck and avoid the blow. In ducking under the counter he dropped his hat but he did not stop to pick it up. Instead, he dashed out of the bar followed by another Australian who wanted to give him a bashing for his disgraceful behaviour towards me. The following evening he was back again, not for his hat but to apologise for, in his own words, his reprehensible behaviour of the previous night. He promised not to insult me again. I accepted his apologies, we shook hands and, believe it or not, we eventually became very good friends. He also became one of my best customers and one of my staunchest supporters, always ready to take my side if need be.

We subsequently discovered that wherever we went we had to go through a trial period before being accepted. We found that we had to live down many ingrained prejudices and popular fallacies. I am happy to say, however, that we have always passed the test with flying colours. There is a quality that I admire about Australians and it is that if you can show them to be wrong they will readily admit it and change their attitude accordingly. They are not stubborn people.

A TALENT FOR BUREAUCRACY

Professor A.F. Davies in Australian Democracy (1958).

The characteristic talent of Australians is not for improvisation, nor even for republican manners, it is for bureaucracy. We take a somewhat hesitant pride in this, since it runs counter not only to the archaic and cherished image of ourselves as an ungovernable, if not actually lawless, people; but, more importantly, because we have been trained in the modern period to see our politics in terms of a liberalism which accords to bureaucracy only a small and rather shady place. Being a good bureaucrat is, we feel, a bit like being a good forger. But in practice our gift is exercised on a massive scale: in the powerful public institutions to be examined presently; in the commercial and industrial monopolies dominating key sectors of the productive process; in the trade union movement, most articulate and tentacular in the world; in corresponding associations of business-men and farmers organised obsessively down to the shavings of shared interest; and even in bodies as superficially unwelcoming as universities, free churches and voluntary associations of all kinds.

Of course, the pervasiveness of bureaucracy is a feature of most industrial societies, and its spread, which has been slow and steady, has its roots not only in developing technology, but also – and especially in its political application – in the modern demand for security and equality. Australian appetites have merely been in a general way larger and coarser than the average, and much more concentratedly political. It is on the supply, rather than the demand, side that Australia has really scored: in particular by the construction in this century of a national government machine, which, thoroughly professional at the core, is nevertheless neither invidiously recruited, nor authoritarian in outlook, but even able, in an odd way, to draw nourishment from its envelope of representative democracy.

*

Most of the government monopolies referred to by Professor Davies have now been sold off and are no longer run by bureaucrats, but a new form of bureaucrat has emerged. Here is the Introduction to Sisters in Suits *(1990) by Marian Sawer.*

In 1988 a visitor to Australia had only to turn to the 'Help' pages of the telephone book in any major city to find a range of services such as women's refuges, domestic violence referral and crisis intervention lines, rape crisis centres, incest centres, women's information lines, abortion counselling and lesbian lines. None of these services was available in 1968. Many widespread social phenomena such as sexual harassment and domestic violence had yet to be named: 'They were just called life.' Over the last twenty years there has been a quiet revolution in Australia. Governments have come to acknowledge some of the reality of women's lives and to address the specific needs of their female citizens. This book tells the story of how Australian feminists came to work through government. It focuses on the unique bureaucratic machinery they developed to achieve their goals.

In the early part of this century, Australia had a reputation as a social laboratory. In the 1980s Australia regained this status – thanks to its feminist reformers. By 1988, even Soviet delegates at UN Committees were requesting that meetings be held to study the Australian experience. As was true of earlier social movements in Australia, the distinctive achievements of more recent Australian feminism have been in the realm of bureaucratic innovation. Over the last fifteen years Australian women have created a range of women's policy machinery and government-subsidised women's services (delivered by women for women) which is unrivalled elsewhere.

This is very much in the Australian tradition, where farmers, businessmen, the labour movement and now Aboriginal and ethnic communities have all looked to the state to service their needs. Characteristically, the term 'femocrat' was to be invented in Australia to describe those feminists who took on women's policy positions in the bureaucracy. This kind of utilitarian attitude towards the state has distinguished the current wave of Australian feminists from those elsewhere, for example, in the United Kingdom and the United States.

OBEDIENT

The historian John Hirst in 'The Distinctiveness of Australian Democracy', (2004).

At my university, at the beginning of each semester, I am asked to speak to the new students from overseas. My task is to tell them what sort of society they have come to. Most of what I say is very conventional and would not surprise you. But one thing I say I ask them to keep secret from the Australians they will meet. I tell them that Australians are a very obedient people.

Australians imagine themselves to be the opposite of obedient. They think of themselves as anti-authority. They love a larrikin. Their most revered national hero is a criminal outlaw, the bush-ranger Ned Kelly. Their unofficial national anthem honours an unemployed vagrant who commits suicide rather than be taken by the police troopers for stealing a sheep.

All this is true. So I am careful to give the evidence for Australian obedience.

We were the first nation to make the wearing of seatbelts in cars compulsory. We have gone further and made the wearing of bike helmets compulsory for the riders not only of motor bikes but push bikes as well.

We led the way with compulsory breath tests for the drivers of motor cars to ensure they are not driving under the influence of alcohol.

Our laws against smoking in public places are very severe. Smoking is banned at our greatest sporting stadium, the Melbourne Cricket Ground – even though it is open to skies. At games of Australian Rules football the spectators yell foul abuse at the umpire and then at half time they file quietly outside to have a smoke.

Australians are suspicious of persons in authority, but towards impersonal authority they are very obedient.

12

Contrasts

Definition is regularly made by contrast. Most of the colonists who came from Britain were proud to be British even while they defined the distinctiveness of their new society by its differences from Britain. Australians no longer think of themselves as British, but are they still more British than they imagine?

AUSTRALIA OR BRITAIN OR ...?

Ethel Richardson (1870–1946), who wrote under the name Henry Handel Richardson, describes the classic case of the unsettled migrant in her novel The Fortunes of Richard Mahony (1930). Mahony was a doctor who came to Australia in the 1850s goldrush; having done well he returned to England against his wife's wishes; and then still dissatisfied he went back to Australia. In England they entertain the best people of the town of Buddlecombe. Mary puts on a large supper in the Australian style; the guests are appalled and almost nothing is eaten. Mahony upbraids his wife for her mistake and she replies as follows.

'Yes, if it's anything to do with yourself, it's preposterous. But when it's me, it's mistakes, and faux pas, and all the rest of it. Sometimes I really feel quite confused. To remember I mustn't shake hands here or even bow here. That in some quarters I must only say "Good afternoon," and not "How do you do?" – and then the other way round as well. That nice Mrs. Perkes is not the thing and ought to be cold-shouldered; and when I have company I'm not to give them anything to eat. Oh, Richard, it all seems to me such fudge! How grown-up people can spend their lives being so silly, I don't know. Out there, you had to forget what a person's outside was like – I mean his table-manners and whether he could say his aitches – as long as he got on and was capable ... or rich. But here it's always: "Who is he? How far back can he trace his pedigree?" – and nothing else seems to matter a bit. I do believe you might be friends with a swindler or a thief, as long as his family-tree was all right. And the disgrace trade seems to be! Why, looked at this way there wasn't any one in Ballarat who was fit to know. Just think of Tilly and old Mr. Ocock. Here they would be put down as the vulgarest of the vulgar. One certainly wouldn't be able to bow to them! And then remember all they were to us, and how fond I was of Tilly, and what a splendid character she had. No, this kind of thing goes against the grain with me. I'm afraid the truth is, I like them vulgar best. And I'm too old, now, to change. You know I'm willing to put up with any mortal thing, as long as I can feel sure you're happy and contented. But when I think, dear, of the down you used to have on narrowness and snobbishness ... And this is even worse.'

'All the same, I felt I could stand no more of the rough diamonds we had to hobnob with out there.'

'Still, some were diamonds, weren't they?'

'What we need, you and I, Mary, is a society that would take the best from both sides. The warm-heartedness of our colonial friends, their generosity and hospitality; while we could do without the promiscuity, the worship of money, the general loudness and want of refinement. – You wonder if I shall be happy here? I like the place, love; it's an ideal spot. I like this solid old house, too: and so far the climate has suited me. I seem to be getting on fairly well with the people, and though the practice is still nothing extraordinary, it has possibilities.'

'Yes, but …'

'But? Well, I undoubtedly miss the income I used to have; there's little money to be made – compared with Ballarat, it's the merest niggling. And besides that, there was a certain breadth of view – that we'd got used to, you and I. Here, things sometimes seem atrociously cramped and small. But we must remember good exists everywhere and in every one, wife, if we only take the trouble to look for it. And since the fates have pitched us here, here we must stay and work our vein until we've laid the gold bare. We've got each other, love, and that's the chief thing.'

'Of course it is.'

MUCH BETTER THAN BRITAIN

The Sydney Morning Herald in 1879 was definite about Australia's superiority for one group.

But it is in regard to the working-classes that the greatest contrast to English every-day life is to be found. To put the matter plainly, the working man here toils less hours, earns higher wages, lives more comfortably, and has more enjoyment than he could possibly hope for at home. Any one who wishes to form an idea of the condition of the working classes here need only notice how they turn out on a holiday – and holidays occur here in a way unknown in England. The recognised and regular holidays are New Year's Day, Anniversary Day (January 26), Good Friday, Easter Monday, Queen's Birthday, Prince of Wales' Birthday, Christmas Day and Boxing Day. All these festivals are most religiously kept, to say nothing of special occasions, such as races, regattas, trade anniversaries, exhibitions, &c., which are eagerly seized upon as opportunities for an outing. There is no place in the world that presents greater facilities for enjoying a holiday than Sydney; there is no place where such facilities are more availed of. On these occasions everybody is early astir, and after an early breakfast crowds of people may be seen wending their way towards the steamer, the train, or other modes of transit to some favourite place of recreation. As a rule they are all well dressed, and the hampers and baskets they carry with them evidence that the solid and substantial elements of enjoyment are not wanting. A pleasant trip in the harbour, or an excursion by rail or omnibus, brings them to the selected scene of the day's pleasure, and then free and unrestrained enjoyment is the order of the day. In the evening all the theatres and other places of amusement are thronged, and the festivities are kept up from beginning to end with unflagging zeal. It is only a people who are fairly prosperous that can afford to enjoy themselves in this way. Nor does the ordinary family life of the working classes evince the presence of that grinding poverty so common at home. The workman here enjoys an amount of independence he is a stranger to in the mother country. With most of the artisans eight hours is a day's work; some trades work nine hours, but ten is the exception. Wages, too, are fairly good, so that the labourer can live in a style that he would have considered luxurious in England. Meat, instead of being a delicacy to be enjoyed only on Sundays, makes its appearance on the table at every meal; bread, butter, cheese, and other viands are within the workman's reach. Fruit is plentiful and cheap, including grapes, peaches, nectarines, apricots, bananas, oranges, and other varieties that in England are generally scarce, and always dear.

WAS AUSTRALIA BETTER?

'Faces in the Street' was one of the first poems written by Henry Lawson, republican, socialist – and born in Australia. He was twenty-one when this was published in 1888.

> They lie, the men who tell us for reasons of their own
> That want is here a stranger, and that misery's unknown;
> For where the nearest suburb and the city proper meet
> My window-sill is level with the faces in the street –
>> Drifting past, drifting past,
>> To the beat of weary feet –
> While I sorrow for the owners of those faces in the street.
>
> And cause I have to sorrow, in a land so young and fair,
> To see upon those faces stamped the marks of Want and Care;
> I look in vain for traces of the fresh and fair and sweet
> In sallow, sunken faces that are drifting through the street –
>> Drifting on, drifting on,
>> To the scrape of hurried feet –
> I can sorrow for the owners of those faces in the street.
>
> In hours before the dawning dims the starlight in the sky
> The wan and weary faces first begin to trickle by,
> Increasing as the moments hurry on with morning feet,
> Till like a pallid river flow the faces in the street –
>> Flowing in, flowing in,
>> To the beat of hurried feet –
> Ah! I sorrow for the owners of those faces in the street.
>
> The human river dwindles when 'tis past the hour of eight,
> Its waves go flowing faster in the fear of being late;

But slowly drag the moments, whilst beneath the dust and heat
The city grinds the owners of the faces in the street –
  Grinding body, grinding soul,
  Yielding scarce enough to eat –
O I sorrow for the owners of the faces in the street.

I wonder would the apathy of wealthy men endure
Were all their windows level with the faces of the Poor?
Ah! Mammon's slaves, your knees shall knock, your hearts in
  terror beat,
When God demands a reason for the sorrows of the street,
  The wrong things and the bad things
  And the sad things that we meet
In the filthy lane and alley, and the cruel, heartless street.

And so it must be while the world goes rolling round its course,
The warning pen shall write in vain, the warning voice grows
  hoarse,
But not until a city feels Red Revolution's feet
Shall its sad people miss awhile the terrors of the street –
  The dreadful everlasting strife
  For scarcely clothes and meat
In that pent track of living death – the city's cruel street.

SURE THEY WERE BETTER

Soldiers and nurses in World War I had first-hand experience of their British counterparts. Here are three Australian soldiers on the Tommies (British soldiers) retreating before the great German advance in early 1918. Historians acknowledge the feats of Australian soldiers in the final battles of World War I, but they speak of the superiority of colonial troops generally.

H.R. Williams

As I tramped at the head of my platoon, the rain driving into our faces and dripping from our steel helmets and greatcoats, saw the crowds of fugitives hurrying past, and from the little band of my command heard whistling, laughter, and jokes, I was vastly proud of being an Australian soldier.

At one of our halts, when a group of middle-aged Tommies from a labour battalion asked for cigarettes and said in awe-inspired voices that it was impossible to stop the Boches – as 'they were coming over in swarms,' I overheard one of my platoon remark to his pal: "Struth, Bill, we'll get some souvenirs now!'

They knew that probably within a few days they would be thrown into a battle against a mighty army flushed with success. Their manner would almost have led one to believe that they were about to participate in a sports meeting.

F.E. Fairweather

Some of the British divisions had been badly broken and we passed a number of derelicts all of whom regarded us with a sort of unwilling admiration, as men going up to do the impossible. It makes one feel proud to be an Australian to see our boys after all this, pass through a village singing. They are magnificent and wherever they go they inspire confidence, both in the Tommies and the French civilians.

Unknown soldier on the retaking of Villers-Bretonneux

'Fini retreat, Madame,' said one of the 'diggers' gruffly, when the leading battalion was halted, and sat cleaning its rifles along the side of the Heilly street. 'Fini retreat – beaucoup Australiens ici.'

*

Here are three nurses comparing British and Australian methods.

Sister Olive Haynes

The English are very strict – seem to have tons of rules and regulations. You mustn't ride in a motor without a passport – can't go anywhere. We are longing to get on to our own hospital with Australians again. The English are very nice and good to us, but they are different, somehow. I suppose we are funny to them, too.

The English think the Canadians are like us – 'utterly lacking in any sense of what is right and proper in the right and proper time.' The English are great on appearances – they are so dead scared of what other people will think and are very subservient to authority.

I'll tell you what I'd like – some Boronia – I wonder if it would be possible to send some along? A man sent me a gum leaf from the Trenches he had had sent him from Australia and it was beautiful – you could smell the Eucalyptus – we were sniffing it all day.

Sister M.R. Thomas

In July 1917 I was transferred to an Australian hospital. It was like getting letters from home to be amongst a staff of Australians again. One thing struck me very forcibly – the vast difference between the British and our own Hospital. The former seemed to me nothing but rules and regulations whilst in the latter was a sense of freedom and there was not the terrible strain of keeping the beds absolutely 'so' and it was great to be able to tell the lads they could sit on their beds and even lie on it if they were tired.

Sister Elsie Tranter

We had to interview Matron (in a British hospital) at 6pm and she tried to 'fix us with a look' telling us a few of the Rules and Regulations – meanwhile our brains were busy wondering how we could evade some of them. We left Matron with a jingle of 'don'ts' for nurses in our ears and feeling that if we met a boy pal and talked with him we would be due for six months in the clink and if we walked with him it would be sudden death.

ARE NATIONAL DIFFERENCES REAL?

Gavan Daws asked this question in his study Prisoners of the Japanese *(1994).*

I began imagining that if human beings were worked and starved and beaten to the point of death, they would be reduced to barely functioning skeletons, scraps of biology, with all the so-called veneer of civilisation flayed out of them, all national culture and character trampled out of them. Not so. The juices crushed out of the POWs were, of course, human in the most fundamental sense but, at the same time, all the way down to starvation rations, 1000 calories a day and less, to 100 pounds of bodyweight and less, to the extremities of degradation, all the way to death, the prisoners of the Japanese remained inextinguishably American, Australian, British, Dutch.

The Americans were the great individualists of the camps, the capitalists, the cowboys, the gangsters. The British hung on to their class structure like bulldogs, for grim death. The Australians kept trying to construct little male-bonded welfare states. These national cultural differences were obvious to everyone in the camps in matters crucial to survival, from discipline, to food gathering, to medical-surgical doctrine on amputation.

What emerges is that much of the life or death behaviour of the POWs was based on national origin, the sum of what men carried with them from the place of their birth and upbringing into prison camp. I would go so far as to say that it was nationality above all that determined, for good or evil, the way POWs lived and died, and often whether they lived or died. In fact, the most surprising and unexpected impression left on me is the force of the inextinguishability of these national cultural ethnic differences and divisions and all the behaviours that went with them, including the most extreme behaviours imaginable. For example, it came as a surprise to me – indeed a shock – to find that of all nationalities who were POWs of the Japanese, only Americans killed each other in captivity.

THE ENGLISH CHARACTER

Australians usually contrast themselves to the high-class 'toffy' Englishman. But most of Australia's founding population came from the working class and lower middle class. George Orwell describes them in his essay 'The Lion and the Unicorn' (1940) and could in part be describing Australians.

Here are a couple of generalizations about England that would be accepted by almost all observers. One is that the English are not gifted artistically. They are not as musical as the Germans or Italians, painting and sculpture have never flourished in England as they have in France. Another is that, as Europeans go, the English are not intellectual. They have a horror of abstract thought, they feel no need for any philosophy or systematic 'world-view'. Nor is this because they are 'practical', as they are so fond of claiming for themselves. One has only to look at their methods of town planning and water supply, their obstinate clinging to everything that is out of date and a nuisance, a spelling system that defies analysis, and a system of weights and measures that is intelligible only to the compilers of arithmetic books, to see how little they care about mere efficiency.

But here it is worth noting a minor English trait that is extremely well marked though not often commented on, and that is a love of flowers. This is one of the first things one notices when one reaches England from abroad, especially if one is coming from southern Europe. Does it not contradict the English indifference to the arts? Not really, because it is found in people who have no aesthetic feeling whatever. What it does link up with, however, is another English characteristic which is so much a part of us that we barely notice it, and that is the addiction to hobbies and spare-time occupations, the *privateness* of English life. We are a nation of flower-lovers, but also a nation of stamp-collectors, pigeon-fanciers, amateur carpenters, coupon-snippers, darts-players, crossword-puzzle fans. All the culture that is most truly native centres round things which even when they are communal and not official – the pub, the football match, the back garden, the fireside and the 'nice cup of tea'. The liberty of the individual is still believed in, almost as in the nineteenth century. But this has nothing to do with economic liberty, the right to exploit others for profit. It is the liberty to have a home of your own, to do what you like in your spare time, to choose your own amusements instead of having them chosen for you from above.

One thing one notices if one looks directly at the common people, especially in the big towns, is that they are not puritanical. They are inveterate gamblers, drink as much beer as their wages will permit, are devoted to bawdy jokes, and use probably the foulest language in the world. They have to satisfy these tastes in the face of astonishing, hypocritical laws (licensing laws, lottery acts, etc. etc.) which are designed to interfere with everybody but in practice allow everything to happen. Also, the common people are without definite religious belief, and have been so for centuries.

The Anglican Church never had a real hold on them, it was simply a preserve of the landed gentry, and the Nonconformist sects only influenced minorities. And yet they have retained a deep tinge of Christian feeling, while almost forgetting the name of Christ.

BRITAIN IN AUSTRALIA

The novelist David Malouf in Made in England (2003) finds much of Britain still in Australia.

My father was born in Brisbane but his family were immigrants, Melkites (Greek Catholics) from Lebanon (still Syria when his parents left in the 1880s). A Rugby League footballer and professional boxer in his youth, later the owner of a small trucking business, he had meant, till he met my mother in his early twenties, to be a priest, and remained a devout Catholic, though my mother was not.

He was passionately Australian, but that his patriotism included strong feelings for England, a place he had no connexion with and had never seen, went naturally, it seemed to me, with what he took up from all these English and Irish and Scots songs he liked to sing. He would have said, I think, that England represented all the things in the world he had grown up in that he most admired and lived by: fair play, decency, manliness, concern for the weak and helpless, a belief that life, in the end, was serious.

I did not think of us as exotic, we were too ordinary, too much like everyone else, for that; and despite the name and the 'background', my father was too Australian. But he did have mates who were different, disaffected in a way that he was not, dissident even. One of my father's friends was a part-time violinist, Lionel Phillips, who spoke of himself, in the German way, as a *Musiker*. A scary figure I found him when I was little, with a mouthful of terrible teeth and a lot of wispy grey hair that flew about on either side of his skull. Occasionally my father would bring him home for tea, and afterwards he would take up the little coffin he kept his fiddle in, slip it out of its crimson sleeve, and play for us, grunting and hissing as he attacked the strings, ferociously double-stopping and stamping time with his boot. He played Fritz Kreisler, which we heard on the wireless, but was, I suspect, disgusted with the middle-brow stuff he was forced to perform, musical comedies and vaudeville shows and the like.

There was also my father's friend Max Julius, who was a big noise in the Communist Party. Through him we went to a showing of the first part of *Ivan the Terrible* at a big fundraising affair at the Town Hall for the Russian war effort, and I had my first encounter with Russian cinema, which I would follow up, a decade later, at the Trades Hall and at the weekly showing of the latest Soviet extravaganza, complete with ear-splitting choral music during the interval, at the Lyric, West End.

What all this represented was a quite different line of interests and affections from the one my father and most other Australians followed.

If some of these fellers chose other affiliations and loyalties, people like my father simply shook their heads, shrugged their shoulders and left them to it. What a man chose to believe and devote his life to was his own affair. Part of the ethos – and this was so deeply British as to be essentially Australian – was that you did not interfere.

13

Fair Go

The term 'fair go' is an Australian invention; it derives from the English 'fair play' and for a long time was used in a similar way to refer to keeping to the rules, treating people equally or giving someone a decent chance. More recently it has come to stand for egalitarianism in society at large. So if Australians believe in the 'fair go' they should be committed, it is said, to a truly egalitarian society. Egalitarianism has been a strong force in our history but because it has different forms and meanings, there is plenty of room for disagreement over whether modern Australia is a 'fair go' society. Significantly no-one will argue against 'fair go' as a principle.

NO 'BUNYIP ARISTOCRACY'

Migrants from Britain in the nineteenth century wanted to escape a society where birth gave privileges; they wanted opportunity to be open to all. In 1853 when William Wentworth proposed that an aristocracy be created in New South Wales to provide for a House of Lords on the English model, there was an uproar. The most effective attack on the plan was made by Daniel Deniehy, a well-educated son of convicts and a radical republican. He spoke at a protest rally in the Victoria Theatre.

I will endeavour to make some of the proposed nobility pass before the stage of our imagination, as the ghost of Banquo walked along in the vision of Macbeth, so that we might have a fair view of these harlequin aristocrats (laughter), these Botany Bay magnificos (laughter), these Australian mandarins (roars of laughter). Let them walk across the stage in all the pomp and circumstances of hereditary titles. First, then, in the procession stalks the hoary Wentworth. But I cannot imagine that to such a head the strawberry leaves would add any honour. (Cheers) Next comes the native aristocrat Mr James Macarthur, he would I assume, aspire to the coronet of an earl, I will call him the Earl of Camden, and I suggest for his coat of arms a field vert, the heraldic term for green – (great cheers and laughter) – and emblazoned on this field would be a rum keg of a New South Wales order of chivalry. There was also the colonial starred Terence Aubrey Murray, with more crosses and orders – not perhaps orders of merit – than a state of mandarinhood. (Loud laughter)

But though their weakness is ridiculous, I can assure you that these pigmies might do a great deal of mischief. They would bring contempt on a country whose interest I am sure you all have at heart, until even the poor Irishman in the streets of Dublin would fling his jibe at the Botany Bay aristocrats.

I am puzzled how to classify them. They could not aspire to the miserable and effete dignity of the grandees of Spain. (Laughter). They had antiquity of birth, but these I would defy any naturalist properly to classify. But perhaps it is only a specimen of the remarkable contrariety that exists at the Antipodes. Here you all know the common water mole was transformed into the duck-billed platypus, and in some distant emulation of this degeneration, I suppose we are to be favoured with a bunyip aristocracy.

OPPORTUNITY FOR THE SMALL MAN

In the 1850s, when hundreds of thousands of gold seekers arrived, most of the good land was in the hands of the squatters, who leased their runs at low rental. The popular cry was that the land be thrown open at cheap rates so that ordinary people could become small farmers. Charles Thatcher gave the land reform movement a song.

> Hurrah for Australia the golden,
> Where men of all nations now toil,
> To none will we e'er be beholden
> Whilst we've strength to turn up the soil;
> There's no poverty here to distress us,
> 'Tis the country of true liberty,
> No proud lords can ever oppress us,
> But here we're untrammelled and free.
>
> Then hurrah for Australia the golden,
> Where men of all nations now toil,
> To none will we e'er be beholden
> Whilst we're able to turn up the soil.
>
> Oh, government hear our petition,
> Find work for the strong willing hand,
> Our dearest and greatest ambition
> Is to settle and cultivate land:
> Australia's thousands are crying
> For a home in the vast wilderness,
> Whilst millions of acres are lying
> In their primitive wild uselessness.
> Then hurrah for Australia, &c.
>
> Upset squatterdom's domination,
> Give every poor man a home,
> Encourage our great population,

And like wanderers no more we'll roam;
Give, in mercy, a free scope to labour,
Uphold honest bold industry,
Then no-one will envy his neighbour,
But contented and happy will be.
Then hurrah for Australia, &c.

NO SNOBBISHNESS

Charles Bean, later the official historian of Australia's part in World War I, in The Dreadnought of Darling (1911) *welcomes the absence of snobbishness.*

In the outside country life, whether pastoral or at the mining camps, is above all things simple. On the land – you go on making money until drought, or pest, or fire, or flood knocks you down, and then you begin again. The demeanour with which he takes those disasters, when they come upon him, is the most lovable thing about the up-country Australian. Day after day news will come in from the paddocks of more cattle dead or dying with the tick pest, or sheep dwindling through want of feed – it is almost always want of feed, not want of water. Everybody knows that 'the boss' must be feeling as if his heart's blood were draining away; and yet from the conversation around the breakfast table you would hardly know there was a tick in Queensland. If things get better they may pull through and start again even stronger than their neighbours; if they get worse the boys may have to go off and work for somebody else, and the girls will enter a tea or flower shop in Sydney or Melbourne; or the old man may perhaps be left by the banks as manager of the run he once owned.

In a country like that it is impossible for money to be a criterion in social position – and the mere possession of money has not a tithe of the admiration which it gets in older countries. I have not known a man or a boy in Australia who showed the least shame-facedness in owning himself poor when he was in rich company – I do not believe even a germ of that feeling exists, and one devoutly hopes it never may. It means there is an almost entire absence in Australia of any striving to keep up the appearance of being richer than you are.

In the same way the fact that, in Australian opinion, any calling is honourable so long as it is honest, is probably due to the ideas of the back country. In the back country, where a man is face to face with nature all the time and fighting her for all he is worth, his success, and indeed his very life, depends on facing the facts – there is no time or use for frills. If a man is a refined and educated man, then he takes the position of one whether he keeps a store, or manages a post office, or a police station, or a sheep run. Without damaging himself socially he can drive a coach or a bullock waggon.

The effect of this pastoral life has always been all against the false incentives and ideals and the whole hopeless crippling bias which are given to life by snobbishness. One could not pretend to claim that there is no snobbishness in Australia; there is a fair amount of it in certain circles. But I think it is not in the sentiment of the people, and there is this powerful influence of the out-back life which may be relied on to fight against it all the time; so that the prospect really seems to be that with the younger generations it may grow less rather than more.

*

Bean was careful to say he was discussing the attitude of men and boys. Charles Dilke, an English visitor of the 1860s, noticed different attitudes between men and women in his Greater Britain (1868).

The first settlers were active, bustling men of fairly even rank or wealth, none of whom could brook the leadership of any other. The only way out of the difficulty was the adoption of the rule, 'All of us to be equal, and the majority to govern', but there is no conception of the nature of democracy, as the unfortunate Chinese have long since discovered. The colonial democrats understand 'democracy' as little as the party which takes the name in the United States; but there is at present no such party in the colonies as the Great Republican Party of America.

Democracy cannot always remain an accident in Australia: where once planted, it never fails to fix its roots; but even in America its growth has been extremely slow. There is at present in Victoria and New South Wales a general admission among the men of the existence of equality of conditions, together with a perpetual rebellion on the part of their wives to defeat democracy, and to reintroduce the old 'colonial court' society, and resulting class divisions. The consequence of this distinction is that the women are mostly engaged in elbowing their way; while among their husbands there is no such thing as the pretending to a style, a culture, or a wealth which the pretender does not possess, for the reason that no male colonist admits the possibility of the existence of a social superior. Like the American 'democrat', the Australian will admit that there may be any number of grades below him, so long as you allow that he is at the top; but no republican can be stauncher in the matter of his own equality with the best.

NO BOSSING

Richard Twopeny in Town Life in Australia (1883) describes how working people expected to be treated.

The Australian working-man is perhaps too well paid to suit us poor folks who are dependent upon him; but, for all that, comfortable means bring an improvement in the man as well as in his condition. It is very trying to have – as I recently had – to go to four plumbers before I could get one to do a small job for me, and still more trying to find the fourth man fail me after he had promised to come. Such accidents are of everyday occurrence in colonial life, and they make one doubt the advantages of a wealthy working-class. But, independent and difficult to please as the colonial working-man is, his carelessness is only a natural consequence of the value set on his labour. Provided he does not drink, you can get as good a day's work out of him as at home. He will pick his time as to when he will do your job, and hesitate whether he will do it at all; but having once started on it, he generally does his best for you. Too often the sudden increase of wages is too much for his mental equilibrium, and a man who was sober enough as a poor man at home, finds no better use for his loose cash than to put it into the public-house till. But as a class I do not think Australian working-men are less sober than those at home. Those who are industrious and careful in a very few years rise to be masters and employers of labour, and are at all times so sure of constant employment that it is no wonder they do not care about undertaking odd jobs. If their manner is as independent as their character, I am far from blaming them for it, though occasionally one could wish they did not confound civility and servility as being equally degrading to the free and independent elector. But when you meet the man on equal terms in an omnibus or on other neutral ground, this cause of complaint is removed. Where he is sure of his equality he makes no attempt to assert it, and the treatment he receives from many parvenu employers is no doubt largely the cause of intrusive assertion of equality towards employers in general.

GOOD WAGES

Leader of the unemployed, Melbourne 1855.

The first and great primary right of all others – the right to live by their labour and support their wives and families in moderate comfort and decent respectability.

*

Justice Higgins in the 'Harvester judgement', 1907.

The test to be applied in ascertaining what are fair and reasonable conditions of remuneration of labour, under the Excise Tariff 1906 is, in the case of unskilled labourers – what are the normal needs of the average employee regarded as a human being living in a civilized community.

ALL THE SAME AFTER THE REVOLUTION?

In 1893 Henry Lawson composed 'For'Ard', an attack on the inequality of wealth and a vision of what might replace it. 'Clown' in the last verse has its old meaning of a simple ordinary person.

> It is stuffy in the steerage where the second-classers sleep,
> For there's near a hundred for'ard, and they're stowed away
>   like sheep –
> They are trav'lers for the most part in a straight 'n' honest path;
> But their linen's rather scanty, an' there isn't any bath –
> Stowed away like ewes and wethers that is shore 'n' marked 'n'
>   draft.
> But the shearers of the shearers always seem to travel aft.

In the cushioned cabins, aft,
With saloons 'n' smoke-rooms, aft –
There is sheets 'n' best of tucker for the first-salooners, aft.

Our beef is just like scrapin's from the inside of a hide,
And the spuds were pulled too early, for they're mostly green
    inside;
But from somewhere back amidships there's a smell o' cookin'
    waft,
An' I'd give my earthly prospects for a real good tuck-out aft –
    Ham an' eggs 'n' coffee, aft,
    Say, cold fowl for luncheon, aft,
Juicy grills an' toast 'n' cutlets – tucker a-lor-frongsy, aft.

What's the use of bein' bitter? What's the use of gettin' mad?
What's the use of bein' narrer just because yer luck is bad?
What's the blessed use of frettin' like a child that wants the
    moon?
There is broken hearts an' trouble in the gilded first saloon!
We are used to bein' shabby – we have got no overdraft –
We can laugh at troubles for'ard that they couldn't laugh at aft;
    Spite o' pride an' tone abaft
    (Keepin' up appearances, aft)
There's anxiety an' worry in the breezy cabins aft.

But the curse o' class distinction from our shoulders shall be
    hurled,
An' the influence of Kindness revolutionize the world;
There'll be higher education for the toilin' starvin' clown,
An' the rich an' educated shall be educated down;
An' we all will meet amidships on this stout old earthly craft,
An' there won't be any friction 'twixt the classes fore-'n'-aft.

We'll be brothers, fore-'n'-aft!

Yes, an' sisters, fore-'n'-aft!

When the people work together, and there ain't no fore-'n'-aft.

RELIANT OR TOO RELIANT ON GOVERNMENT

Australians came to expect that the government would provide them with 'fair and reasonable' conditions. The historian Keith Hancock describes the Australian approach to government in his 1930 book Australia.

Australian democracy has come to look upon the State as a vast public utility, whose duty it is to provide the greatest happiness for the greatest number. The results of this attitude have been defined as *le socialisme sans doctrines*. Its origins, however, are individualistic, deriving from the levelling tendency of migrations which have destroyed old ranks and relationships and scattered over wide lands a confused aggregate of individuals bound together by nothing save their powerful collectivity. Each of these individuals is a citizen, a fragment of the sovereign people; each of them is a subject who claims his rights – the right to work, the right to fair and reasonable conditions of living, the right to be happy – from the State and through the State.

To the Australian, the State means collective power at the service of individualistic 'rights.' Therefore he sees no opposition between his individualism and his reliance upon Government.

*

There was a minority view – grown stronger in recent times – that Australians were too reliant on government. Henry Wrixon, a long-serving member of the Victorian parliament, made this the subject of his novel Jacob Shumate (1903).

The first thing that attracted the attention of the new MP, when he came down to breakfast a few mornings after election day, was the large heap of letters that lay upon the table awaiting his attention.

He was surprised to find what a number of Cricket Clubs, Rowing Clubs, Tennis Clubs, Racing Clubs, Hare and Hound Clubs, and General Sports Committees were anxious to do him honour.

Then there were the letters which came from people who had learned to cherish a comprehensive trust in their Government. The settlers in the Cote Cote Valley wrote to ask when the Government was going to drain their land; or were they to leave the land after the Government had put them on it? The members of the Tum Tum Fox Club informed the Member that the Department had sent them down rifles to help to destroy the foxes, but where was the ammunition? Did they expect them to kill the foxes without? An indignant parent complained that he did not get the full allowance of sixpence a week per child for bringing his children to school over the limit fixed by law for the allowance – though the road was so bad that he had to put a pair of horses in the trap to carry them. A comparatively poor widow wanted a place for her daughter as a typist, or something respectable, as she could barely make ends meet now with the price of things and the high wage for the house-help. The Art Association of Brassville wanted slight assistance from the Government, or somebody, to enable one of their members to make a painting of the charming copy of Raphael's 'La Giardiniera' that was in the Public Gallery of Miranda.

WHAT'S THE MEANING OF 'FAIR GO'?

In 2004 Peter Saunders of the Centre for Independent Studies took objection to many policies that were urged as being necessary to provide a 'fair go'. He examined what Australians meant by the term.

All Western liberal democracies recognise the importance of the principle of 'fairness', but Australia probably emphasises it more than most. Our belief in the 'fair go' has evolved to become part of our national culture, even though it is not entirely clear what this term means.

In the mid-nineteenth century, a 'fair go' seems to have referred mainly to the importance of opening up opportunities so that everyone could compete. It was consistent with what today we think of as a meritocratic ideal. In the early decades of federation, however, governments increasingly pursued a national agenda intended to blur social divisions and build a strong sense of belonging and sameness, and the 'fair go' ideal in this period came to be identified with the political manipulation of distributional outcomes associated with an egalitarian ethic. This national interventionist strategy has, however, been in retreat for 30 years or more (although it remains relatively strong in the area of social policy), and survey evidence demonstrates that most Australians today have a much broader understanding of 'fairness' than mere egalitarianism.

The 'fair go' today still recognises the ideal of equalising outcomes, but it also encompasses the competing ideals of meritocracy (reward for effort and talent) and fair exchange (the liberal principle of the right to private property provided it has been acquired in accordance with the rule of law). The egalitarian definition of fairness, which is taken for granted by the social policy intelligentsia as the only relevant definition, does not therefore do justice to what most Australians mean by a 'fair go' in the contemporary period. Indeed, if our social affairs intellectuals and pressure groups ever got their way, and taxes and welfare benefits were both raised even higher than they are at present in order to narrow what they call the 'income gap', the result would be the very opposite of what most Australians think a 'fair go' entails.

IS THE 'FAIR GO' OPERATING?

Both major parties have largely abandoned the controls over wages, markets and trade, which had been used to secure 'fair and reasonable' conditions. Carmen Lawrence of the Labor Party thinks the 'fair go' is slipping away. John Howard, the Liberal prime minister, claims he is still guided by this principle among others.

Carmen Lawrence

As a member of the Labor Party, I have always been passionately committed to egalitarianism – the idea that each person has equal worth; that any limitations on their achievement and their ability to share in society's goods should be systematically broken down. And that this requires public action and investment.

The conservatives embrace – if they do at all – a pallid version of equal opportunity. They think it is enough to let people step up to the mark and do as well as they can no matter what handicaps they start with. They speak from the vantage point of privilege, blind to their own advantages. They fail to understand that promoting equal opportunity actually requires active intervention to minimise disadvantage and ensure that people's life chances are more equal; so that the accident of your birth does not cripple your future.

Most Australians still hold firm to the view that ours is an egalitarian society. Indeed, there are some who argue that egalitarianism is the value that defines us. While more of us are uneasy about the widening income and wealth gaps we see, many still appear to accept the boast made by our leaders that ours is a nation of equals where the ethic of a 'fair go' is the norm governing our private and public relations. But is this really so?

There is now a great deal of evidence which challenges this comfortable assertion. While researchers may disagree about the extent of the problem, they generally agree that inequality amongst

Australians is increasing and that egalitarianism itself may be under threat as a defining social objective. And they all agree that it matters.

I was recently asked to review three new books on the subject of inequality and poverty and I was struck by the fact that although they use different data sources and levels of analysis, all three reached the same conclusion. We are a less equal society than we have ever been.

Fred Argy, in his book *Where To From Here?* argues that Australia's distinctive form of egalitarianism evolved over 70 years through institutional regulatory and policy mechanisms, a form of 'state paternalism', defined by a commitment to a strong role for government in advancing human wellbeing.

The historic roots of our egalitarian ethic lie in a pragmatic commitment to sharing the wealth of the country and the benefits of productivity, particularly through the award- and wage-fixing system – the 'wage-earners welfare state'. One of the features of this 'settlement' was a recognition that government could be – and should be – a major player in achieving equality. Argy details 'seven pillars' which were deliberately created by government action:
-   the virtual guarantee of full-time employment,
-   the protection of wages and conditions of workers,
-   an unconditional needs-based welfare safety net,
-   a strongly progressive tax system,
-   generous government provision of non-cash benefits such as education, health and housing,
-   a balanced distribution of regional economic opportunities and
-   the capacity for workers to be involved in workplace decisions affecting their wellbeing.

Argy's systematic analysis of the extent of erosion of these pillars and the reasons for the decline he identifies makes sobering reading.

John Howard

We believe, as we always have, that 'the only real freedom is a brave acceptance of unclouded individual responsibility'.

And in making policy since we took office, that encouragement of self-reliance, of giving people choice, of rewarding those who can and do take responsibility for themselves and their families has been at the forefront of our efforts.

Australians are in step with the times – they have and always will place great store in encouraging independence, initiative, of individuals being accountable to themselves.

For instance, the community has overwhelmingly accepted the value of mutual obligation, and in particular 'working for the dole'. Not to punish young people anaesthetised by passive welfare but to develop their skills and awaken an enthusiasm for independent life. The facts speak for themselves – over 91,000 participants involved in 4000 community projects. Eighty-four per cent believe that their involvement has been worthwhile, improving their skills and restoring their morale.

Similarly, the Tough on Drugs Diversion Programme offers a foothold for young drug offenders sliding down towards lifetime addiction and crime – but only if they're prepared to take personal responsibility for their recovery.

The far-reaching and fundamental changes to industrial relations law give back power to individual workers.

The incentives for private health insurance encourage people to accept responsibility for their own family's health.

The child-immunisation programme encourages parents to protect their own children.

The changes to education funding improve the choices available to parents.

Our support for self-funded retirees, for share ownership, for first-home buyers, for elderly Australians wishing to remain in their own homes longer – all these initiatives have as their foundation, a desire to empower and enrich the lives of individual Australians – to make and keep them self-reliant.

And yet whilst self-reliance is an ambition being pursued throughout the world, the Australian way also emphasises a balance with the other principles we hold dear.

And the second of those is to ensure equality of opportunity and equality of treatment, of 'doing the right thing' and ensuring that all Australians are given a 'Fair Go'.

This nation was built on the principle that whatever you earn, whatever your starting point, each one of us is owed a chance to succeed. Each one of us has a right to health, education and opportunity. And each one of us deserves a leg up if times get tough.

For this reason, we have held as immutable an unwavering commitment towards both Medicare and the social security safety net. Despite my political opponents' attempt to portray the Government as forsaking those in need, the reality is we've sought to lift them out of isolation and hardship. I resolved, as Prime Minister, to provide a modern welfare system – not one entrenched in the past – which embraces prevention as much as it affords cure.

We have avoided the relative harshness of the American approach where the needy can often be left penniless. Yet we've eschewed the excessive paternalism of some European societies, which leave individuals dependent on bloated and unsustainable public sectors.

THE ESSENCE OF IT

Craig McGregor in Profile of Australia *(1966) saw egalitarianism as most evident in the style of social interaction. Forty years ago he saw this casual égalité as under threat, but correctly forecast its survival.*

Egalitarianism, in fact, is the persistent motif which runs through Australian culture and the people themselves. One can say many things about Australians: that they are individualistic, informal, easy-going, frank, good-natured – all more or less correct, though there are many Australians who are none of these things – but the feeling that one man is as good as another is the most characteristic quality of social relations, and as an ideal it has power over executive and working man alike. George Nadel, the historian, has argued that Australian nationality is defined by this 'social ethic' rather than anything else: 'The attempt to discover common ground for the members of a new society issued in the search for a unity whose attainment was and is to be evidenced in the social relations of man.' Australians are generally free of the extreme forms of snobbery, rudeness, and deference which are the outward signs of social antagonism in older countries. The bus driver and conductor regard themselves as equal to any of their passengers, and are treated as such. The skilled tradesman regards himself as every bit as good as the white-collar worker, and sometimes gets paid more. The subtle distinctions in the behaviour of people of one class to another which bedevil European social relations are comparatively absent in Australia.

Often the first thing visitors notice about Australia is this apparent classlessness and social equality: the easy relations which exist between people of all walks of life, the absence of gross privilege, the pleasant sense of camaraderie. ('I am struck by something indisputably *gentle* about Australia,' said Dame Edith Sitwell during her visit in 1963.) This casual *égalité* is really rather misleading (Australia is not a classless society but one in which most people have gravitated towards the middle), but it exists nonetheless. Even the wealthy feel under pressure to be accepted by ordinary working Australians, rather than the other way around; if the plumber calls to mend the sink it's imperative to offer him a cup of tea, and I know one or two well-spoken people who automatically adjust their accent to the company in case they should be thought 'affected'. Australians sit beside the taxi driver on the front seat, drift easily between public and saloon bar in the pub, dislike tipping because it implies a servile relationship. Domestic help is almost impossible to obtain for the same reason. It is the land where nobody calls you 'Sir' (except sometimes out of politeness), where arrogance is the worst sin and deference the next. The Australian likes to call no man his master and likes to think of no man as his servant.

In recent years this egalitarianism has begun to crumble before the pressures generated in post-war Australian society: affluence, competitiveness and the spread of middle-class values have taken their toll. As the middle class has become the dominant social group in Australia so its attitudes and beliefs have begun to replace the old working-class ones.

And yet those who forecast that Australians will lose their habit of equality altogether underestimate the persistence of old ways and old attitudes through times of change. Finally, there is the tradition of equality itself. It is so strongly entrenched in Australia that it will take decades of more intensive social stratification than is now going on to wipe it out altogether. Australians, at home or overseas, feel that they should conform to the national stereotype of the rough, friendly, democratic Australian who has been glorified in a hundred books, poems, yarns and anecdotes. The result can be seen any day of the week in Earls Court, London or once every four years at the Australian Olympic team's billet: a raucous, shoulder-slapping group of Aussies strenuously acting out the national myth and determinedly proving themselves even more Australian than the Australians back home. Australians take it for granted that they are friendly, gregarious, unsnobbish people, and because they believe it they usually are.

14

Humour

Humour is revealing of national character, a quick way into what is otherwise difficult to define.

ANTIPODES

James Mudie wrote The Felonry of New South Wales (1837) to discredit Governor Bourke, who was attacked by conservatives for being too favourable to convicts and ex-convicts. Mudie wanted to show that the convict colony was truly a world turned upside down. He tells this story to shock — and amuse. Laughter was one way of accepting the bizarre nature of convict society and the disdain of outsiders. Mudie appears as His Honour because he was a magistrate. The young man in the story (who receives the mock classical name Celebs) was passing Mudie's gate en route to Sydney to choose a wife from the convicts at the Female Factory when he was told that on Mudie's property there was a woman who might suit. She was the very pregnant Marianne.

MARIANNE: I wish to ask you a favour, your honour.

His Honour: Why, Marianne, you have no great reason to expect particular indulgence; but what is it?

MARIANNE: [*curtsying and looking still more interesting*]: I hope your honour will allow me to get married.

His Honour: Married! To whom?

MARIANNE: [*rather embarrassed*]: To a young man, your honour.

HIS HONOUR: To a young man! What is he?

MARIANNE: [*her embarrassment increasing*]: I really don't know!

HIS HONOUR: What is his name?

MARIANNE: I can't tell.

HIS HONOUR: Where does he live?

MARIANNE: I don't know, your honour.

HIS HONOUR: You don't know his name, nor what he is, nor where he lives! Pray how long have you known him?

MARIANNE: [*her confusion by no means over*]: Really, to tell your honour the truth, I never saw him till just now. Mrs Parsons sent for me to speak to him; and so, – we agreed to be married, if your honour will give us leave. It's a good chance for me. Do, your honour, give me leave!

HIS HONOUR: Love at first sight, eh! Send the young man here.

[*Exit Marianne*]

[*Enter Celebs*]

HIS HONOUR: Well, young man, I am told you wish to marry Marianne, one of my convict servants.

CELEBS: [*grinning*]: That's as you please, your honour.

HIS HONOUR: As I please – Why, have you observed the situation the young woman is in? [*Marianne being 'in the way ladies wish to be who love their lords.'*]

CELEBS: [*grinning broadly*]: Why, your honour, as to that, you know, in a country like this, where women are scarce, a man shouldn't be too '*greedy*'! I'm told the young woman's very sober, – and that's the main chance with me. If I go to the factory, why, – your honour knows I might get one in the same way without knowing it, – and she might be a drunken vagabond besides! As to the piccaninny, if it should happen to be a boy, you know, your honour, it will soon be useful, and do to look after the pigs.

THE GREAT AUSTRALIAN JOKE

Charles Bean recorded this joke in The Dreadnought of the Darling *(1911) for the benefit of British readers; he assumed all Australians already knew it.*

It is the story of the sad and final breach between two mates who had been carrying their swags in company for some time along the interminable road that leads always to the horizon. Early one morning, up a creek-bed to the side of them, they passed a big black object which, whatever it was, had clearly been dead some days. About midday Bill took his pipe out of his mouth. 'D'jer see that dead ox?' he grunted. The shadows of evening were closing around them, when Jim spat solemnly into the camp fire. ''Tweren't an ox. 'Twas a 'orse,' he said. After that he turned in and slept eight well-deserved hours. When he awoke there was no sign of Bill or Bill's swag. Bill was clearly gone. Only a grimy note was left stuck in a cleft stick. 'There's too much argyment in this here camp,' it said.

IRONY

Brian Matthews, a considerable humorist himself, gives this as a true story in the 'Humour' entry in The Oxford Companion to Australian History *(1998) to illustrate the ironic national style.*

The scene is a grassy flat with a ramshackle shed in the background overhung by tall stringybarks. A battered tractor, on the carry-all of which are stacked several huge newly cut lengths of redgum, stands alongside an equally disreputable utility truck with its tray sides down. It is obvious that the redgum 'strainer' posts have to be transferred to the ute; it is equally obvious that the two men who are leaning on the bonnet of the ute are contemplating this very problem. Eventually, one of them – the one with the bush hat, check shirt, scrubby moleskins and a perpetual cigarette pasted to his lips through the smoke of which he squints and coughs – decisively begins to give directions to the other, the better-dressed, rather 'city' looking one. Following these directions but clearly having failed to understand them, he backs the ute at a certain angle to the logs on the tractor; it is the wrong angle. He is given more directions and moves the ute to a different but patently still wrong position. With every bone and angle of his body exuding massive tolerance, the man in the moleskins issues more instructions, supplementing his words with a number of choice expletives and much waving and pointing. This time, the driver gets it right and positions the truck, after which, hopping down from the driver's cabin, he gives an embarrassed grin and says: 'Sorry Tom – there can't be many more wrong ways of doing that!' Deadpan, lips scarcely moving, voice emerging in a nasal, smoky, saturnine drawl, the man in the moleskins says, 'Well, I dunno – I reckon you would've found a few, given time.'

LACONIC COURAGE OF EXPERIENCE

During his stay in Australia in 1922, D.H. Lawrence was very taken by the weekly magazine the Bulletin, then past its great days (it began in 1880) but still printing amusing anecdotes sent in by readers. Lawrence examined them in Kangaroo. Richard Lovat Somers, the central character, is loosely based on Lawrence himself.

Somers liked the concise, laconic style. It seemed to him amusing without trimmings. Put ship-shape in the office, no doubt. – Sometimes the drawings were good, and sometimes they weren't.

LADY (*who has just opened door to country girl carrying suitcase*): I am suited. A country girl has been engaged, and I'm getting her tomorrow.

GIRL: I'm her, and you're not. The 'ouse is too big.

There, thought Somers, you have the whole spirit of Australian labour.

SUCRE: Peering through her drawing-room window shortly before lunch, the benevolent old suburban lady saw a shivering man in a ruined overcoat. Not all the members of the capitalist classes are iron-souled creatures bent on grinding the faces of the afflicted, yet virtuous poor. Taking a ten-shilling note from a heavily-beaded bag, she scribbled on a piece of paper the words: *Cheer Up*, put both in an envelope, and told the maid to give it to the outcast from her. While the family was at dinner that evening a ring sounded at the front door. Argument followed in the hall between a hoarse male voice and that of the maid. 'You can't come in. They're at dinner.' 'I'd *rather* come in, miss. Always like to fix these things up in person.' 'You can't come –' Another moment, and the needy wayfarer was in the dining room. He carefully laid five filthy £1 notes on the table before his benefactress. 'There you are, mum,' he said, with a rough salute. 'Cheer Up won all right. I'm mostly on the corner race days, as your cook will tell you; an' I'd like to say that if any uv your *friends* –'

Bits, bits, bits. Yet Richard Lovat read on. It was not mere anecdotage. It was the momentaneous life of the continent. There was no consecutive thread. Only the laconic courage of experience.

TO SHOCK AND AMUSE

Craig McGregor in Profile of Australia (1966) explains a double aspect of humour.

Australians use bad language (when it is not just a matter of habit) for two purposes: humour and shock. The two are closely connected, because much Australian humour is based upon the shock tactic: the most typical jokes are those which both revolt and amuse at the same time, or use bizarre exaggeration to produce a sort of wry half-disgusted reaction in the listener. The Australian sense of humour is often called sardonic, which is true enough, but it is not so often realized that this sardonic quality often extends to the joke-teller himself, so that he stands detached from the joke and often seems to laugh at himself for telling it; the joke is merely a shock device which neither the listener nor the teller takes seriously. Unfortunately most examples are unprintable, but many Australian jokes about, for example, Jews or women might shock an outsider as being unforgivably vicious or obscene, whereas an Australian would see its blatant viciousness or obscenity as part of its humour. Australians are often sending themselves up even when they seem to be taking themselves most seriously; the terse, ironic comment is as much a feature of pub conversation as of Australian poetry.

15

Newest Australians

The great migration program since 1945 has brought millions of foreign observers who have developed their interpretations of Australia while making their lives here and in contrast to what they have left behind.

HIGHLY CULTIVATED HUNGARIAN COUPLE

Andrew Riemer writes about his parents and himself in Inside Outside: Life between Two Worlds (1992).

As our cousin's car made its way through streets that, by European standards, were empty and drained of life, we began to wonder where the real city, the centre of its life, might be found. In *The Road from Coorain*, Jill Ker Conway writes eloquently about her first visit to Seville. She was amazed, and enchanted to discover its great civic spaces – the cathedral, the plaza, the university – around which the life of the city turned. Here was something absolutely alien to her experience of city life – restricted as it had been to Sydney, Melbourne and Newcastle – an urbanity the like of which Australia could not provide. Though I could not have recognised it at the time, our first impression of Sydney was the direct opposite of the awakening that young Australian woman was to experience in Seville – we could find no physical, spiritual or social centre in a city which seemed to contradict all our notions of what urban life should be.

For my parents, initially at least, Australia was paradise. It may have been a curious and perplexing place, but it offered considerable safety and very little menace. If the worst that could happen to you was to have 'Go home, bloody ref!' shouted at you in the street, then the worst was good enough. The boring blandness of suburban Sydney was the guarantee they had been seeking. Surely, you could never have concentration camps in a place like this. Australia was a haven, a blessed land that seemed miraculously to have escaped the evils and the horrors of the old world.

For that reason, despite a sense of strangeness and perplexity, my parents were only too prepared to admire the world in which they had chosen to live; they were eager in their desire for acceptance. They knew in their heart of hearts that they would never become more than passably proficient in English. They also came to realise that they would always hanker after the world they had lost – a world which, they reminded themselves, had ceased to exist in 1939: a world, moreover, where they had witnessed brutality of a sort that could not possibly exist in these enlightened modern times, or so they had imagined. In their eyes, assimilation became not something imposed on them by a threatening hostile society, but a desired goal, an aspiration which could never, alas, be fulfilled.

Along with that desire, bred out of gratitude and a sense of relief, went an unrecognised but, I think, deeply felt wish for something which was in essence nothing other than the desire for oblivion, the annihilation of the personality. This disturbing state of mind arose because they were only too conscious of what, in later years, was to become a recurring theme for discontent – the strangeness of Australia, an unfamiliar society which they came to regard as culturally impoverished. If only they could forget what they had lost. If only the past, the good together with the appalling, could be wiped out, then surely happiness and contentment would be theirs. They wanted to be remade, knowing all along what an impossible desire that was. They could not, of course, be refashioned. Freedom and security was theirs, and that was almost enough to compensate. Yet it was not quite enough. Though willing to become Australians – even if that were to prove impossible – those old habits, the familiar comforts of a very different world, could not ultimately be suppressed.

My parents grew, at length, to understand why Australians were not given to dancing in the streets, why their great ideal was to own a house with heavily curtained windows. Yet they never lost the feeling, which I have inherited from them, that this was a land of sleepwalkers.

ITALIANS, COMING AND GOING

Morag Loh collects accounts of Italian migrant experience in With Courage in Their Cases *(1980).*

Grazia
We've been back to Italy twice in the sixteen years since we were married. Last time we took the children. I was happy to see my friends again but many have gone from my town, emigrated to other parts of Europe. In Germany and France mostly. I've never been homesick for Italy. My parents haven't been either. The first years you are so busy to work you don't have time, you don't go out, you don't speak English, you have worries in the family. Life here is completely different and you are busy getting used to it. It takes you about twenty years. When I went to Italy two years ago me and my friends were on the same level. I had changed but people have changed there too. They don't work hard because there's no work for women like here, but they're happy. You have less work and money but a better life in some ways.

Here in Australia if you don't work you don't get in touch with people. People don't come in and out, you don't see your neighbours, you miss people, you get depressed. If you stay home you go mad. You got to get interested in something. But I'm not sorry I left Italy. I worked hard before my children were born to help buy a block of land and when our son was born we started to build. My husband worked hard, including every weekend, for a long time to pay off the house. But now we're free and can go out with friends and family at the weekends to picnics. We can think about building a little holiday house at the beach. My husband is very good. He's always helped me in the house. It's not usual for Italian men. Especially if they were born over there they think they're kings. My husband came here by himself, without his parents, that's why he's like that. I'm lucky. I have my home, my husband and my children. I'm happy here.

My kids often ask me, 'Mum, what am I? Italian or Australian?' I say, 'You're Australian because you were born here, but you got Italian parents and you speak two languages.' But they feel they're Italians. Even though they are born here they say they're Italians. They're pleased about it, very pleased.

Franco

When we came here for me things were alright. I got an Australian certificate, I had qualifications, I found work. But six months later my wife started to become ill. She was very nervous, crying day and night, walking in her sleep, talking in her sleep.

She had nobody here – no parents, brothers, sisters. In our hometown she didn't work, but here, to help me, she found work in a factory. It was very hard for her as it was piece work. She was under great pressure. She felt exhausted, she was homesick all the time. I work with women, Italians, Greeks, Yugoslavs, and many of them are homesick. Eighty per cent have mental problems everything is so different here.

My wife felt very isolated and was upset very often. She couldn't read English and didn't even want to try. She cried always and wanted to go home. Three years later, the doctor said, 'I can do nothing. It's better if you go home to Italy.' So I sold everything to pay for our passage on the boat and we departed.

My wife was very happy but I wasn't. I liked it in Australia because I found there wasn't a great deal of competition in my field of work. In Australia, if the hairdressing business goes badly there was the opportunity to find employment in a factory or a hotel. In Italy it would be too shameful for me to do that. A hairdresser washing dishes in a hotel kitchen or working as a labourer? Impossible! It was better here in that respect, there was more freedom in the choice of work.

In Italy everyone goes out all the time. There is pressure put upon you to go too. 'I'm going here, there … want to come?' It's difficult to say no. But for that you need money. In the morning, everyone goes to the espresso bar for coffee and brioche. When you go for lunch you also have an aperitif, like a *Campari*. You spend and spend. In Australia nobody does this. Most people have two sandwiches. I still keep to the Italian custom, so every day I have four or five coffees, but still I don't spend money like I did in Italy.

Soon, we were going out every weekend, we were never home. That is the life you lead there and you spend and spend. You have to. Soon I was complaining to my wife, 'I want to go back to Australia. Life is a bit easier there. I have more opportunity to work. I can work part-time at night and there's not the constant pressure to go out and spend. Our family will be better off.'

At that time many working people in Italy had money and not just because of the boom. Some lived in government apartments, similar to Housing Commission flats, and the rent was very cheap. Others lived with their mother or mother-in-law. That was a cheap way of living too. But by now I had different mentality and didn't like to live with parents or hear commotion in the street. I was a bit like an immigrant in my own country.

My wife never wanted to return here but in 1970 we did come back. To get money to open a shop, I worked six months in a stocking factory. Then, until business picked up, I worked at night making nuts and bolts. I was glad to be back. My wife is still sick but she isn't as bad as before. I am not an Australian citizen because in fifteen years, when I finish work, I plan to go back to Italy. This is the best thing for my wife and it will be the only reason, because for me, Australia is all right.

Rosalba

I'm happy to be going back to Italy after two years here but I've gained a lot in Australia. I gained some of the Anglo-Saxon culture, especially through university. I gained a lot of experience in what it means to be a migrant in a new country. Not new as being in a new place, but because Australia is only two to three hundred years old from a European point of view. I know what it's like to be isolated from the mainstream of your own culture, what it's like to work really hard. And to be completely influenced by a consumeristic society. Italy still has some agricultural traditions, artisan traditions, but there isn't only the agrarian society and the working class, the official culture is in touch with political life, it influences the working class. I don't mean that one is more important than the other, they all contribute to make Italy different from here. Here it's straight out capitalist culture. You work hard for those consumer goods. In Italy you might earn less, live in a smaller place, but you take life more easy. The thing that amazed me was how often people changed house here. When you've got a house what are you looking for another one for? It's the society that makes them that way, keeping up with the Joneses. People work hard in Italy too, but it's harder here because there's just work. No discussion groups. No *passeggiata*.

Passeggiata is not just walking up and down the street, it's meeting people, discussing things with them, you talk. 'You see what that party did?' 'I think the other's better?' 'What about the soccer?' 'What about the film?' It's communication.

Valeria

We went back feeling Italian, but we found that we're Australian Italians somehow and we didn't feel at home as we thought we would. We've developed here independently, we speak differently, we've become more self-contained, more disciplined, more reserved. It was a shock. So unexpected.

Everywhere, even in Turin, people jump the queue in shops. They just go up to the front to be served, never say, 'Oh, you're first,' You have to say, 'I'm next,' elbow your way through, speak up. And Italians bargain. You do it here, at the food market with Italian stall-holders, but in Italy you bargain for clothes too in many places, especially street stalls. I'm very Anglo-Saxon, I'm disciplined, I obey the queue. And I'm not very sharp. I like prices on things because I know they shoot the price up and down according to the customer. But after a while I learnt to bargain. It's an act. You go into a shop, murmur, 'Too dear, too dear,' and they knock a few lire off. If you hold back, or are timid, they think you're soft in the head. I knew our relatives would be happy to see us, but I really felt that over there, people in the streets, people in general, would welcome you with open arms. But that didn't occur. I think I must have been idealistic, having a lot of illusions. I thought I was going back to where I really belonged but unfortunately I don't belong there.

And we found we couldn't express our affection as openly as our relatives. We could cry but never so long or so freely. There's a sort of reserve in us now, we keep our distance from people at first.

When people ask me what I am I never say Australian and I
don't think I ever will. That's not to say I'm not proud to be an
Australian citizen. Of course if you say you're Australian, kids say
'No you're not Miss. Where were you born? What's your surname?'
But that's not what stops me from saying, 'I'm Australian'. I just
can't. It would be negating what I am. I'm an Italian who belongs
here. What upsets me sometimes is that so many Australians are
going to Italy, marrying Italians, settling there and becoming Italians. They've got all the culture under their noses. It's mine but I
can't have it. I know that what I've been proud of being, I cannot
fully be.

VIETNAMESE WHO LEARN FROM ITALIANS

*Nguyen Xuan Thu collects Vietnamese experiences of migration in Life
with Past Images (1986).*

Dai Trang Dinh

We also learned from the experiences of our Italian neighbours.
They told us that when they came to Australia, they came with
only a small bag of possessions and a mind which had not been
equipped with appropriate knowledge and professional skills to
cope with the new society. But now, nearly 30 years later, they own
their own large business. All this showed us that not only people
who had high academic achievements could be successful in Australian society.

My father usually took the example of our Italian neighbours
to distinguish the values of Australian society and Vietnamese
society. In the old Vietnamese society, it was very difficult for a
person who was not highly educated to be successful and respected
by society. On the other hand, in Australian society, people only

need to have some professional skills and to know how to work hard and then they can succeed easily and live a happy life.

When still in Vietnam, we all planned that when we came to Australia, we would continue to study until we became well qualified, because at that time we thought that was the best road for us to take in order to have a secure future. But after seeing the example of our neighbours, my brother and I began to see there are two choices for the future: one is to prepare to become an intellectual with a high degree, and the other is to train for a number of skills.

My parents are letting us have the freedom to choose our future. They do not want to have hopes of higher education for their children and then be disappointed as has happened in a number of other families. However, in the depth of their heart, we know what our parents really want for us. So at this time, my brother and I are assessing our capabilities in order to choose the best road for our future.

A HOLOCAUST SURVIVOR FROM POLAND

Maria Lewitt records her experiences in No Snow in December *(1985).*

Our children are simply Australians and I am grateful to Australia for their uncomplicated lives. It's their home, and has been ours for almost a lifetime. I am still learning how to cope with certain democratic practices which were difficult to accept, like police protection offered to extreme political organisations, like the right to criticise, to state openly and loudly whatever one wants.

We have royal commissions and though they take a long time, they exist, and not even a member of parliament, not even a member of the police force, can abuse the system without it being noticed.

We have settled in a country where more money is spent on sport and gambling in a week than on all the arts put together throughout the year. We are living in a country where the fire brigade is willing to rescue a cat from a tree, or a dog from a drain. The money we spend on food for our pets in a week would support a family in less fortunate countries for months. We Walk for Want. We are progressively more conscious of the wider issues.

We do think about the future and the bomb, even though not as often as we do about our own comfort, and often without fully realising the close connection between the two.

The fact that I prefer rye bread to a sandwich loaf doesn't keep me apart from my countrymen any more. I still can't understand how cricket or football can evoke passion, admiration, and draw huge crowds. On the other hand, my children and grandchildren can't understand why I can't understand.

We seldom make world news, but lucky is the country that doesn't.

Long gone are the days of my pregnancy, when I longed for a Polish forest. The Australian gums and I have become good friends since and, for a change, I missed their rugged beauty while staying in Europe, away from home.

We enjoy barbecues, bush-walking – but, above all, that unique feeling of freedom one can enjoy only in a democracy.

16

Going Native

The boldest claim in the long business of assessing the Australian character is that Aboriginal culture has had a profound effect on the culture of the people who invaded their country. At the conclusion of her book Dancing with Strangers (2003) Inga Clendinnen wrote, 'Through processes I do not yet understand, we are now more like each other than we are like any other people.' These extracts deal with the coming together of two cultures.

LEARNING BUSH SKILLS

Russel Ward in The Australian Legend (1958) identified an Aboriginal influence on the bushmen ('the nomad tribe' of pastoral workers) at a time when Aborigines were usually not mentioned in the history books.

Finally, in proportion as the later bushmen felt themselves to be the 'true Australians', there are hints that they felt too some indebtedness to the Aborigines. This is not to say that the remaining black men in the 1880s and 1890s were admitted to the ranks of the nomad tribe, but simply that many bushmen felt themselves to be, in some sense, the heirs to important parts of Aboriginal culture. After all, no white man has ever been the equal of the Aborigines in essential bush skills, in tracking, finding water, living on bush food, and so on. And it is doubtful whether white men have ever equalled

Aborigines in some purely European-derived arts, such as horse-breaking or cattle-mustering. In the early days many a lost white man, and child, owed his life to the charity of the dark people, and even now they are still called upon whenever a white man is lost in the bush. If, as has been argued, the bushman's esprit de corps sprang largely from his adaptation to, and mastery of, the outback environment, then the Aborigine was his master and mentor.

There is, of course, overwhelming evidence that the usual overt attitude to the Aborigines continued to be almost as brutal and contemptuous at the end of the nineteenth century as it had been earlier, but underlying this attitude and qualifying it, there grew up, often in the same person, an awareness of indebtedness to the first nomads who had come to terms with the difficult land. There are some hints, in the ballads and elsewhere, that after the Aborigines had ceased to be dangerous to even the loneliest swagman, folk-memory tended to acknowledge, perhaps to sentimentalize, this indebtedness which, like so many other components of the up-country outlook, has since become a commonplace attitude in Australian literary work.

Hemmed in by the vertical sandstone cliffs of the Blue Mountains on the floor of the valley of Mangrove Creek, there live to-day descendants of earlier Australians, both black and white. The two races have inter-married and along 'the Crick' men distinguish one family from another by speaking of the white or black Smiths, Joneses or Hogans, but all alike talk respectfully at times of 'the Old People' whose paintings may still be seen on the walls of lonely caves which, tradition says, were later used by bushrangers and cattle-duffers.

The feeling is reflected faithfully in 'The Stockman's Last Bed', one of the most continually popular bush ballads of the last century, and one of the few possessing traces of genuine poetic power. Vance Palmer's version of the relevant stanza reads:

His whip is silent, his dogs they do mourn,
His nag looks in vain for his master's return:
No friend to bemoan him, unheeded he dies,
Save Australia's dark children none knows where he lies.

THE GREAT AUSTRALIAN GAME

Australian Rules Football is a local invention, first played in Melbourne in the late 1850s. There has been a long argument over whether the Aborigines had an influence on the distinctive style of the game. The consensus is that they did not, but David Thompson, a young scholar, has recently strengthened the claim for Aboriginal influence in 'Origins of the Australian Football Code' (2005). Two important shapers of the early Melbourne rules, Tom Wills and Henry Harrison, had close connections with Aborigines.

Indigenous Australians traditionally played football. Although there were regional variations of the sport, usually a contest was played between two teams and often each team had a leader. The people of one locality would play another or the people belonging to a particular totem would contend against those belonging to another. Interestingly two common totems were eagle and crow – the eagles have been playing against the crows for hundreds if not thousands of years. Many people participated though numbers varied, presumably depending on the availability of players. Up to 200 people played a single ball game near Swan Hill. In western Victoria a round ball was made from possum pelts with the fur on the outside wrapped around crushed charcoal, which gave the ball weight. In Gippsland the Kurnai made the ball from a kangaroo scrotum stuffed with grass. At Coranderrk near Healesville, the ball was made of 'twine formed of the twisted hair of the opossum'.

A game could last many hours and the contenders played with sense of fun rather than competitive spirit, though in western Victoria the best player earned the honour of 'burying the ball in the ground' until later required.

According to the nineteenth-century amateur anthropologist James Dawson, allied and akin Aboriginal groups in western Victoria played a traditional form of football in which:

> Each side endeavours to keep possession of the ball, which is tossed a short distance by hand, and then kicked in any direction. The side which kicks it oftenest and furthest gains the game. The person who sends it highest is considered the best player.

Reverend Bulmer observed a traditional game played by the Kurnai in which the ball was 'thrown, or kicked up with the foot. Whoever catches the ball oftenest, wins the game'. The Kaurna around Adelaide played Parndo, taken from the name of the 'flattish' possum skin that served as the ball. If the ball fell to the ground a player lifted it up and passed it to another player who then kicked the parndo into the air to be caught. The Kulin of central and southern Victoria played Marngrook. A player did not throw the ball 'as a white man might do, but drops it and at the same time kicks it with his foot, using the instep for that purpose' which describes a punt-like kicking action.

The first games of Australian football were being played while Aboriginal people continued to play indigenous football only a few kilometres away. According to McFarlane and Roberts' *Collingwood at Victoria Park*, as late as 1862 the Wurundjeri were:

> often seen … in their possum skin coats, armed with spears, and retreating mainly to the unsold hill north of Colling-

wood where they camped with their dogs, played football
with a possum-skin ball and fought with other Aborigines.

Apparently many Melburnians had the opportunity to witness
indigenous football. The Aborigines at Coranderrk near Healesville also played football during the 1860s which Europeans witnessed. Considering the vast region of south-east Australia where
indigenous football was played, it is possible that many early footballers observed Aboriginal games.

An Aboriginal team maintained possession by kicking, catching and throwing the ball. The Melbourne rules encouraged possession by allowing a free kick for a fair catch and 'a succession of
good well-directed kicks, to the hands of those the ball was intended
for'. Indigenous and early Australian football both permitted the
ball to be kicked in any direction to team-mates. The Victorians
had a preference for punt and drop kicks; punt-style kicks predomi-
nated in indigenous football. Aboriginal players leaped high in the
air to catch the ball from a kick and high marking featured in Australian football no later than 1862. In England soccer-style kicking
was preferred and ball catching restricted. The evidence suggests it
is possible, even likely that some early footballers, impressed with
the indigenous game may have experimented with local skills, in
particular jumping high into the air to catch the ball. There is also
strong evidence that Wills was introduced to the indigenous game.
If he was influenced by indigenous football it would help explain
why the rules encouraged the kicking and catching game, why off-
side was ignored and why jumping high in the air featured early in
the game. Later Harrison, who had also been friendly with Aboriginal people, helped revise the rules, the code maintaining the key
features of the Melbourne club game under his authority.

AN ABORIGINAL NATION

Germaine Greer, the Australian feminist, suggested in Whitefella Jump Up (2003) that 'the shortest way to nationhood' for Australians was for them to imagine themselves as Aborigines, which was not, she claimed, so outlandish a proposition because there were already great similarities between the two peoples.

The common perception from within the country is that white Australians and black Australians are very different. Outsiders are rarely in a position to assess the family resemblance between the two groups, but I for one am struck by the degree of influence exerted by Aboriginal people on the formation of the Australian character and way of life. Australians, despite the official policy of multiculturalism, aren't genuinely cosmopolitan, but they aren't British either. They exhibit neither British manners nor British values. If Australians should doubt this, they have only to travel to England, where they will feel less at home than they would in any other part of the world. Their gestures are too ample, their voices too loud, their approach too direct and their spontaneity embarrassing. Their lack of class consciousness mystifies the English who are obsessed by calculations of relative status, and inordinately anxious to avoid the kind of gaffe that would betray inferiority. Australians are amused by the number of times English people will say 'please' and 'thank you' either, when 'gibbit' will do. Even Australians who gradually learn to mute their responses and respect the Englishman's desperate need to believe that he is alone in the midst of a crowd will not succeed in passing as British; after thirty years' residence in the country, I am still startled by taxi-drivers and their ilk asking me how long I've been over there and when I am going home. People who should know better ask me whether I think the way I do because I come from barbarous and backward Australia. And I probably do, but I'm damned if I'll give them the pleasure of hearing me say it.

Australians cannot be confused with any other Common-wealth peoples; they behave differently from Canadians, South Africans and even New Zealanders. It is my contention, diffidently offered, that the Australian national character derives from the influence of the Aborigines whose dogged resistance to an imported and inappropriate culture has affected our culture more deeply than is usually recognised. From the beginning of colonisation, the authorities' deepest fear was that settlers would degenerate and go native. In many subtle and largely unexplored ways they did just that.

In the way we behave, the way we speak, the way we feel about lots of things, white Australians exhibit the effects of the gentle but insistent and pervasive influence of black Australia, passed down through our culture as surely as white genes passed into the black genome. The more we try to deny it, the more the inextricability of black and white will become obvious, if not to Australians them-selves then certainly to outsiders. This is our badge of hope; we should wear it with pride.

THE LAND MAKES US ONE

In his best-selling book The Future Eaters *(1994), a history of Australia through deep time, Tim Flannery considers how the harsh land influenced both the peoples who have lived on it.*

It is easy for contemporary, urban Australians to forget the impor-tance of the social bonds inherent in the ideal of mateship. After all, most of the time people are busy trying to live their lives away from the scrutiny of their near neighbours and to avoid the petty conflicts that arise as a result of living in such close proximity. But the Australian environment will not permit even urban Australians to escape indefinitely from the difficulties faced by the pioneers. The Sydney bushfires of January 1994 are a good example, but ENSO-spawned flood and fire have, at one time or another, devastated parts of virtually every major Australian city. In such circumstances, mateship suddenly re-emerges *en masse* in the suburban wilderness and people do extraordinary things to help those whose lives have been affected.

During the Sydney bushfires I witnessed one such event. Real estate agents are not often known for their sense of morality, but on the morning following the fire I saw an agent locate a new flat to rent, for a single mother who had lost everything, and give her $1300 in open cheques to cover her initial costs. The Commonwealth Bank – another institution not usually known for its generosity – opened its doors over the weekend, suspending housing repayments, arranging emergency funding and acting as a depot for donations. Neighbours, many of whom rarely spoke to each other, were working side by side to help clean up. Others were discreetly handing over cash to those more drastically affected than themselves. So many opened their homes to those whose houses had been burned that there was no shortage of accommodation. As a result – in contrast to the aftermath of the Los Angeles earthquake of 19 January 1994 – there was no tent city, indeed not a single tent in Sydney following the fires. For the people of places like Jannali, the prospect of a tent city housing their neighbours would have been a deep insult to their sense of mateship. They would have done anything in order to avoid it.

I find it both intriguing and heartening that European Australians should seize upon the ideal of mateship so quickly after colonising their new home. That it should persist for so long in an environment as adverse as the sprawling Australian suburbs is little short of a miracle. Such caring is the very sweetest of the uses of adversity. Perhaps there is something quite fundamental about such social obligations that makes them indispensable in the Australian environment. There is no doubt that Aboriginal culture, particularly as it existed in the more hostile environments, had this sense of sharing. Aborigines had, and indeed still have, social obligations which link people over thousands of kilometres. In times of crisis, these social obligations could see people sharing their few resources with visitors from even more severely affected areas. It is perhaps a tribute to the harshness of Australian environments that these two human groups, which are so different in many other ways, should both develop and maintain such an onerous system of social obligation and sharing.

ABORIGINAL HUMOUR

Germaine Greer in Whitefella Jump Up *and Inga Clendinnen in* Dancing with Strangers *both claimed that there is a similarity in Aboriginal and settler Australian humour. Here are two Aboriginal jokes.*

Mosquito was an Aborigine in New South Wales who agreed to hunt bushrangers in Tasmania to escape imprisonment on Norfolk Island. He eventually joined up with Tasmanian Aborigines in the bush and was condemned to death for shooting a settler. This exchange occurred in Hobart gaol.

MOSQUITO: Hanging no good for blackfellow.

GAOLER: Why not as good for a blackfellow as for whitefellow if he kills a man?

MOSQUITO: Very good for white fellow, for he used to it.

*

In the 1930s Depression it was a common saying that 'We should give the land back to the blacks.' This was one response of the Aborigines, as recorded by Richard Broome in Aboriginal Victorians (2005).

White boy he now pays all taxes
Keep Jacky Jacky in clothes and food
He don't care what becomes of the country
White boy's tucker him pretty good

CHORUS
Clicketa Boobilah wildy maah
Billying etcha gingerry wah

Now the country's short of money
Jacky sits and laughs all day
White boy wants to give it back to Jacky
No fear, Jacky won't have it that way

His Country – After All

Henry Lawson embodies his criticism of Australia and his love for it in the one story, set in New Zealand.

The Blenheim coach was descending into the valley of the Avetere River – pronounced Aveterry – from the saddle of Taylor's Pass. Across the river to the right, the grey slopes and flats stretched away to the distant sea from a range of tussock hills. There was no native bush there; but there were several groves of imported timber standing wide apart – sentinel-like – seeming lonely and striking in their isolation.

'Grand country, New Zealand, eh?' said a stout man with a brown face, grey beard, and grey eyes, who sat between the driver and another passenger on the bus.

'You don't call this grand country!' exclaimed the other passenger, who claimed to be, and looked like, a commercial traveller, and might have been a professional spieler – quite possibly both. 'Why, it's about the poorest country in New Zealand! You ought to see some of the country in the North Island – Wairarapa and Napier districts, round about Pahiatua. I call this damn poor country.'

'Well, I reckon you wouldn't, if you'd ever been to Australia – back in New South Wales. The people here don't seem to know what a grand country they've got. You say this is the worst, eh? Well, this would make an Australian cockatoo's mouth water – the worst of New Zealand would.'

'I always thought Australia was all good country,' mused the driver – a flax-stick. 'I always thought –'

'Good country!' exclaimed the man with the grey beard, in a tone of disgust. 'Why, it's only a mongrel desert, except some bits round the coast. The worst dried-up and God-forsaken country I was ever in.'

There was a silence, thoughtful on the driver's part, and aggressive on that of the stranger.

'I always thought,' said the driver, reflectively, after the pause – 'I always thought Australia was a good country,' and he placed his foot on the brake.

They let him think. The coach descended the natural terraces above the river bank, and pulled up at the pub.

'So you're a native of Australia?' said the bagman to the grey-beard, as the coach went on again.

'Well, I suppose I am. Anyway I was born there. That's the main thing I've got against the darned country.'

'How long did you stay there?'

'Till I got away,' said the stranger. Then, after a think, he added, 'I went away first when I was thirty-five – went to the islands. I swore I'd never go back to Australia again; but I did. I thought I had a kind of affection for old Sydney. I knocked about the blasted country for five or six years, and then I cleared out to Frisco. I swore I'd never go back again, and I never will.'

'But surely you'll take a run over and have a look at old Sydney and those places, before you go back to America, after getting so near?'

'What the blazes do I want to look at the blamed country for?' snapped the stranger, who had refreshed considerably. 'I've got nothing to thank Australia for – except getting out of it. It's the best country to get out of that I was ever in.'

'Oh, well, I only thought you might have had some friends over there,' interposed the traveller in an injured tone.

'Friends! That's another reason. I wouldn't go back there for all the friends and relations since Adam. I had more than quite enough of it while I was there. The worst and hardest years of my life were spent in Australia. I might have starved there, and did do it half my time. I worked harder and got less in my own country in five years than I ever did in any other in fifteen' – he was getting mixed – 'and I've been in a few since then. No, Australia is the worst country that ever the Lord had the sense to forget. I mean to stick to the country that stuck to me, when I was starved out of my own dear native land – and that country is the United States of America. What's Australia? A big, thirsty, hungry wilderness, with one or two cities for the convenience of foreign speculators, and a few collections of humpies, called towns – also for the convenience of foreign speculators; and populated mostly by mongrel sheep, and partly by fools, who live like European slaves in the town, and like dingoes in the bush – who drivel about "democracy", and yet haven't any more spunk than to graft for a few Cockney dudes that razzle-dazzle most of the time in Paris. Why, the Australians haven't even got the grit to claim enough of their own money to throw a few dams across the watercourses, and so make some of the interior fit to live in. America's bad enough, but it was never so small as that ... Bah! The curse of Australia is sheep, and the Australia war cry is Baa!'

'Well, you're the first man I ever heard talk as you've been doing about his own country,' said the bagman, getting tired and impatient of being sat on all the time. 'Lives there a man with a soul so dead, who never said – to – to himself ... I forget the darned thing.'

He tried to remember it. The man whose soul was dead cleared his throat for action, and the driver – for whom the bagman had shouted twice as against the stranger's once – took the opportunity to observe that he always thought a man ought to stick up for his own country.

The stranger ignored him and opened fire on the bagman. He proceeded to prove that that was all rot – that patriotism was the greatest curse on earth; that it had been the cause of all war; that it was the false, ignorant sentiment which moved men to slave, starve, and fight for the comfort of their sluggish masters; that it was the enemy of universal brotherhood, the mother of hatred, murder, and slavery, and that the world would never be any better until the deadly poison, called the sentiment of patriotism, had been 'educated' out of the stomachs of the people. 'Patriotism!' he exclaimed scornfully. 'My country! The darned fools; the country never belonged to them, but to the speculators, the absentees, land-boomers, swindlers, gangs of thieves – the men the patriotic fools starve and fight for – their masters. Ba-a!'

The opposition collapsed.

The coach had climbed the terraces on the south side of the river, and was bowling along on a level stretch of road across the elevated flat.

'What trees are those?' asked the stranger, breaking the aggressive silence which followed his unpatriotic argument, and pointing to a grove ahead by the roadside. 'They look as if they've been planted there. There ain't been a forest here surely?'

'Oh, they're some trees the Government imported,' said the bagman, whose knowledge on the subject was limited. 'Our own bush won't grow in this soil.'

'But it looks as if anything else would –'

Here the stranger sniffed once by accident, and then several times with interest. It was a warm morning after rain. He fixed his eyes on those trees.

They didn't look like Australian gums; they tapered to the tops, the branches were pretty regular, and the boughs hung in shipshape fashion. There was not the Australian heat to twist the branches and turn the leaves.

'Why!' exclaimed the stranger, still staring and sniffing hard. 'Why, dang me if they ain't (sniff) Australian gums!'

'Yes,' said the driver, flicking his horses, 'they are.'

'Blanky (sniff) blanky old Australian gums!' exclaimed the ex-Australian, with strange enthusiasm.

'They're not old,' said the driver; 'they're only young trees. But they say they don't grow like that in Australia – 'count of the difference in the climate. I always thought –'

But the other did not appear to hear him; he kept staring hard at the trees they were passing. They had been planted in rows and cross-rows, and were coming on grandly.

There was a rabbit trapper's camp amongst those trees; he had made a fire to boil his billy with gum-leaves and twigs, and it was the scent of that fire which interested the exile's nose, and brought a wave of memories with it.

'Good day, mate!' he shouted suddenly to the rabbit trapper, and to the astonishment of his fellow passengers.

'Good day, mate!' The answer came back like an echo – it seemed to him – from the past.

Presently he caught sight of a few trees which had evidently been planted before the others – as an experiment, perhaps – and, somehow, one of them had grown after its own erratic native fashion – gnarled and twisted and ragged, and could not be mistaken for anything else but an Australian gum.

'A thunderin' old blue-gum!' ejaculated the traveller, regarding the tree with great interest.

He screwed his neck to get a last glimpse, and then sat silently smoking and gazing straight ahead, as if the past lay before him – and it *was* before him.

'Ah, well!' he said, in explanation of a long meditative silence on his part; 'ah, well – them saplings – the smell of them gum-leaves set me thinking.' And he thought some more.

'Well, for my part,' said a tourist in the coach, presently, in a condescending tone, 'I can't see much in Australia. The bally colonies are –'

'Oh, that be damned!' snarled the Australian-born – they had finished the second flask of whisky. 'What do you Britishers know about Australia? She's as good as England, anyway.'

'Well, I suppose you'll go straight back to the States as soon as you've done your business in Christchurch,' said the bagman, when near their journey's end they had become confidential.

'Well, I dunno. I reckon I'll just take a run over to Australia first. There's an old mate of mine in business in Sydney, and I'd like to have a yarn with him.'

Acknowledgements

David Brown of the Curriculum Corporation was in charge of this project for the Australia Day Council; I am greatly indebted to him for his tact and support. Chris Feik of Black Inc. saw the worth of the project when it was faltering. He and Black Inc.'s staff have again made book production a pleasure for me. I have been guided to documents by other collectors, particularly Manning Clark and Frank Crowley. Many colleagues have helped me with suggestions: Bain Attwood, Geoffrey Blainey, Judith Brett, Richard Broome, Janet Butler, James Curran, Steve Eather, Bill Gammage, Ian Hancock, Terry King, Marilyn Lake, Andrew Lemon, Morag Loh, Corinne Manning, Keith Pescod, David Potts and Barry Smith. Jeremy Sammut actively pursued documents and showed himself again to be an excellent research assistant. To all my thanks.

J. H.

Sources

Because of the constraints of space, occasionally sentences have been omitted within an extract, or extracts have been composed from non-contiguous paragraphs. These emendations are not indicated in the extract as it has been reproduced. The full text can be consulted in the sources listed below.

Page references below indicate where extracts are not continuous. That is, pp. 12–13 refers to a continuous extract over two pages; pp. 12, 13 indicates a non-continuous extract with quotations from both pages.

The stories and poems of Henry Lawson and the poems of A.B. (Banjo) Paterson are readily available in numerous editions of their work.

Where works have gone through several editions, the chapter rather than the pages numbers are given.

1. *Who Are the Australians?*
Captain Cook's Journal, reproduced in Manning Clark, *Sources of Australian History*, Oxford University Press, London, 1957, pp. 51, 52–3, 54–5.
Robert Lyon, *An Appeal to the World on Behalf of the Younger Branch of the Family of Shem*, printed by J. Spilsbury and J. M'Eachern, Sydney, 1839, pp. 53, 55, 84.
Bigge, John, *Report of the Commissioner of Inquiry into the State of the Colony of New South Wales*, Agriculture and Trade, House of Commons, London, 1823, reproduced in C.M.H. Clark, *Select Documents in Australian History 1788–1850*, Angus & Robertson, Sydney, 1950, p. 434.
Edward Geoghegan, 'The Boy in the Cabbage-Tree Hat', from *The Currency Lass*, ed. Roger Covell, Currency Press, Sydney, 1976, pp. 61–2.
George Meudell, 'Australia for the Australians', *Melbourne Review*, vol. 7, October 1882.

Rolf Boldrewood, *Robbery under Arms: a story of life and adventure in the bush and in the Australian goldfields*, Remington, London, 1888, chapter 1.

'White Australia Policy', *Bulletin*, 2 July 1887.

J.T. Patten and W. Ferguson, *Aborigines Claim Citizen Rights: a statement of the case for the Aborigines Progressive Association*, Publicist, Sydney, 1938.

Arthur Calwell, ministerial statement on immigration, 1945, reproduced in John Lack and Jacqueline Templeton (eds), *Bold Experiment: a documentary history of Australian immigration since 1945*, Oxford University Press, Melbourne, 1975, pp. 20–1.

Catherine and Ronald Berndt, *The First Australians*, Ure Smith, Sydney, 1952, Introduction.

Al Grassby, 'A Multi-cultural Society for the Future', 1973, reproduced in John Lack and Jacqueline Templeton (eds), *Bold Experiment: a documentary history of Australian immigration since 1945*, Oxford University Press, Melbourne, 1975, pp. 143–4.

Jimmy Chi and Kuckles, *Bran Nue Dae*, Currency Press Pty Ltd, Sydney, 1991, pp. 15–16.

Patricia Grimshaw, Marilyn Lake, Ann McGrath & Marian Quartly, *Creating a Nation*, Australian Research Institute, Curtin University of Technology, Perth, 2006, Introduction.

Council for Aboriginal Reconciliation, Draft Document for Reconciliation, 3 June 1999, Council for Aboriginal Reconciliation Archive, <www.austlii.edu.au/au/other/IndigLRes/car/1999/9/>.

2. Independent Spirit

Russel Ward, *The Australian Legend*, Oxford University Press, Melbourne, 1958.

John Sidney, *A Voice from the Far Interior of Australia: by a bushman*, Smith-Elder, London, 1847, pp. 24, 26.

Francis Adams, *Fortnightly Review*, August 1891; *The Australians: a social sketch*, T. Fisher Unwin, London, 1893, pp. 165–6.

William Howitt, *Land, Labour and Gold: or, two years in Victoria with visits to Sydney and Van Diemen's Land*, Lowden, Kilmore, 1972, pp. 310, 374–5.

Anthony Trollope, *Australia*, eds P.D. Edwards & R.B. Joyce, University of Queensland Press, Brisbane, 1967, pp. 449–50.

Miles Franklin, *My Brilliant Career*, William Blackwood and Sons, Edinburgh, 1901, chapter 23.

Ned Kelly's words in the dock, *Argus,* 30 October 1880.

3. *Mateship*

John Chandler, *Forty Years in the Wilderness*, ed. Michael Cannon, Loch Haven Books, Main Ridge, 1990, pp. 90, 91–2, 94.

Rolf Boldrewood, *Shearing in the Riverina 1865*, John Ferguson, Sydney, 1983, pp. 31–3.

T.G.H. Strehlow, *Journey to Horseshoe Bend*, Rigby, Adelaide, 1969, pp. 58–9.

Song about Chinese shearers, reproduced in Russel Ward, *The Australian Legend*, Oxford University Press, Melbourne, 1958, p. 123.

Miriam Dixson, *The Real Matilda: woman and identity in Australia 1788 to the present*, UNSW Press, Sydney, 1999 (Penguin 1976 edition: p. 81).

Macgregor Duncan et al., *Imagining Australia: ideas for our future*, Allen & Unwin, Crows Nest, 2004, pp. 17–19.

4. *Diggers*

Ellis Ashmead-Bartlett, *Argus,* 8 May 1915.

Charles E.W. Bean, 'End of the first phase of the campaign', in *The Official History of Australia in the War of 1914–1918*, vol. 1: The story of Anzac, Queensland University Press in association with the Australian War Memorial, Brisbane, 1981. The 11th edition of the work can be found at <www.awm.gov.au/histories/volume. asp?conflict=1>.

Round Table, March 1919.

Alan Seymour, *One Day of the Year*, in *Three Australian Plays*, Penguin, Ringwood, 1985, pp. 78–80.

Mark Ryan (ed.), *Advancing Australia: the speeches of Paul Keating*, Big Picture Publications, Sydney, 1995, pp. 287–8.

Peter Kieseker, 'Non-government organisations' in *Peacekeeping: challenges for the future*, ADF Academy, Canberra, 1993, pp. 70–3.

Peter Cosgrove in Patrick Lindsay, *The Spirit of the Digger: then and now*, Pan Macmillan, Sydney, 1993, pp. 39–40.

John Birmingham, *A Time for War: Australia as a military power,*
Quarterly Essay 20, Black Inc., Melbourne, 2005, pp. 52–3, 54–5, 55.

5. Larrikins

John Stanley James, *The Vagabond Papers: sketches of Melbourne life,*
in light and shade, third series, 1877, reproduced in Frank Crowley, *Colonial Australia 1875–1900,* Nelson, Melbourne, 1980, p. 33.

C.J. Dennis, *The Songs of a Sentimental Bloke,* Angus & Robertson,
Sydney, 1915.

C.J. Dennis, *The Moods of Ginger Mick,* Angus & Robertson, Sydney,
1916.

Eric Lambert, *The Twenty Thousand Thieves,* Newmont, Melbourne,
1951, pp. 93–5, 145–6.

Sol Encel, 'The Larrikin Leaders' in *Nation,* 25 May 1968.

6. Suburban Nation

Robin Boyd, *Australia's Home: its origins, builders and occupiers,* Melbourne University Press, Melbourne, 1952, pp. 3–4.

George Johnston, *My Brother Jack,* Collins, London, 1964, chapter 13.

Barry Humphries, *A Nice Night's Entertainment,* Currency Press Pty
Ltd, Sydney, 1981, pp. 15–17.

Craig McGregor, *Profile of Australia,* Hodder & Stoughton, London,
1966, chapter 14.

Janet McCalman, *Struggletown: public and private life in Richmond,*
1900–1965, Hyland House, South Melbourne, 1998, p. 54.

Tim Winton in *Good Weekend,* 27 August 1994.

Hugh Stretton, *Ideas for Australian Cities,* published by the author,
Adelaide, 1970, pp. 14–16, 20–1.

7. Empty and Flat

Beatrice Webb, *The Webbs' Australian Diary 1898,* ed. A.G. Austin, Sir
Issac Pitman & Sons, Melbourne, 1965, pp. 107–8.

D.H. Lawrence, *Kangaroo,* Thomas Seltzer, New York, 1923, chapter 14.

Warren Roberts et al. (eds), *The Letters of D. H. Lawrence,* vol. 4,
Cambridge University Press, Cambridge, p. 271.

G.H. Cowling, 'The Future of Australian Literature', *Age,* 16 February
1935.

A.D. Hope, 'Australia' in *The Penguin Book of Australian Verse*, selected and edited by John Thompson, Kenneth Slessor & R.G. Howarth, Penguin, Middlesex, 1958.

Patrick White, *Voss*, Viking Press, New York, 1957, chapter 2.

Donald Horne, *The Lucky Country*, Penguin, Ringwood, 1964, pp. 34–6.

Anna Couani, *Were All the Women Sex-mad? and other stories*, Rigmarole Books, Melbourne, 1982, pp. 29–30. The full text is available at <http://seacruise.ath.cx/annacouani/wereallwomen/Index.html>.

8. *Put-downs*

Charles Darwin, *A Naturalist's Voyage: journal of researches into natural history and geology of the countries visited during the voyage of H.M.S. Beagle under the command of Capt. FitzRoy, R.N.*, John Murray, London, 1879, p. 444.

F.G. Clarke, *The Land of Contrarieties: British attitudes to the Australian colonies, 1828–1855*, Melbourne University Press, Carlton, 1977, p. 170.

Charles Dickens, *David Copperfield*, Chapman, London, 1850, chapter 51.

English cricketer, *Sydney Morning Herald,* 10 February 1879.

Anthony Trollope, *Australia*, eds P.D. Edwards & R.B. Joyce, University of Queensland Press, Brisbane, 1967, pp. 375–6.

J.A. Froude, *Oceana: or, England and her colonies*, Longmans, Green & Co., London, 1886, p. 191.

Oscar Wilde, *The Importance of Being Earnest: a trivial comedy for serious people*, Samuel French, London, 1895, Act II.

Warren Roberts et al. (eds), *The Letters of D. H. Lawrence*, vol. 4, Cambridge University Press, Cambridge, p. 263.

H.G. Wells, *Age*, 27 January 1939.

Lord Moran, *Winston Churchill: the struggle for survival, 1940–1965*, Constable, London, 1966, p. 21.

David Horner, *Crisis of Command: Australian generalship and the Japanese threat, 1941–1943*, Australian National University Press, Canberra, 1978, pp. 209, 210.

Germaine Greer, *London Observer*, 1 August 1982.

Paul Keating, *Age*, 17 November 2005.

Bob Hawke, *The Hawke Memoirs*, Heinemann, Melbourne, 1994, p. 501.

9. Sport

John O'Brien, *Around the Boree Log and Other Verses*, Angus & Robertson, Sydney, 1921.

Richard Twopeny, 'Amusements', in *Town Life in Australia*, Elliot Stock, London, 1883.

Mark Twain, *Mark Twain in Australia and New Zealand*, Penguin, Ringwood, 1973, pp. 161–3.

Daily Telegraph (Melbourne), 27 February 1883.

David Malouf, *Made in England: Australia's British inheritance, Quarterly Essay 12*, Black Inc., Melbourne, 2003, pp. 60–1.

Laurence Le Quesne, *The BodyLine Controversy*, Unwin, London, 1983, pp. 70–1, 72. Reprinted by permission of Random House Group Ltd.

BBC Sport, *Dream Symbol for a New Australia*, BBC Sport website, 15 September 2000, <http://news.bbc.co.uk/sport1/hi/olympics 2000/926700.stm>.

10. Anthems Official and Unofficial

'Advance Australia Fair', 1879 version, National Library of Australia, <http://nla.gov.au/nla.mus-an24220024>.

Dorothea Mackellar, 'My Country', in *The Closed Door and Other Verses*, Specialty Press, Melbourne, 1911.

C.J. Dennis, 'The Australaise', in *Backblock Ballads and Other Verses*, Coles Book Arcade, Melbourne, 1913.

11. Surprises

Richard Twopeny, 'Amusements', in *Town Life in Australia*, Elliot Stock, London, 1883.

Geoffrey Blainey, *Our Side of the Country: the story of Victoria*, Methuen Haynes, North Ryde, 1984, pp. 93–4.

Hatice Hurmuz and Vecihi Basarin, *The Turks in Australia: celebrating twenty-five years in Australia*, Turquoise Publications, Melbourne, 1993, pp. 43, 69, 91, 114.

Osvaldo Bonutto, *A Migrant's Story: the struggle and success of an Italian-Australian 1920s–1960s*, University of Queensland Press, Brisbane, 1994, pp. 45–6.

A.F. Davies, *Australian Democracy: an introduction to the political system*, Longmans-Green, London, 1958, part I, chapter 1.

Marian Sawer, *Sisters in Suits: women and public policy in Australia*, Allen & Unwin, Sydney, 1990, pp. xiv–xv.

John Hirst, 'The Distinctiveness of Australian Democracy', *Papers on Parliament*, Department of Senate, Canberra, 2004. Can be viewed at <www.aph.gov.au/Senate/pubs/pops/pop42/hirst.pdf>.

12. *Contrasts*

Henry Handel Richardson, *The Fortunes of Richard Mahony*, Heinemann, London, 1930, book II, chapter 5.

'Much Better than Britain', *Sydney Morning Herald*, 17 September 1879, reproduced in Frank Crowley, *Colonial Australia 1875–1900*, Nelson, Melbourne, 1980, pp. 65–6.

Charles E.W. Bean, *The Official History of Australia in the War of 1914–1918*, vol. 5, Queensland University Press in association with the Australian War Memorial, Brisbane, 1981, pp. 175, 177. The 11th edition of the work can be found at <www.awm.gov.au/histories/volume.asp?conflict=1>.

Bill Gammage, *The Broken Years: Australian soldiers in the great war*, Australian National University Press, Canberra, 1974, p. 227.

'*We Are Here, Too': the diaries and letters of Sister Olive LC Haynes, November 1914 to February 1918*, compiled and edited by Margaret O. Young, Australian Down Syndrome Association, Adelaide, 1991, pp. 149, 155.

Sister M.R. Thomas, narrative, Australian War Memorial, 41/1052.

Sister Elsie Tranter, diary, State Library of Victoria, MS 10786, pp. 121–2.

Gavan Daws, *Prisoners of the Japanese: POWs of World War II in the Pacific*, Scribe Publications, Carlton North, 2004, Author's Note.

George Orwell, 'The Lion and the Unicorn', in *The Penguin Essays of George Orwell*, Penguin, London, 1984, pp. 146–7.

David Malouf, *Made in England: Australia's British inheritance*, *Quarterly Essay 12*, Black Inc., Melbourne, 2003, pp. 16, 17, 18, 20.

13. *Fair Go*

Daniel Deniehy, speech, reproduced in C.M.H. Clark, *Select Documents in Australian History 1851–1900,* Angus & Robertson, Sydney, 1955, pp. 341–2 (rendered into direct speech).

Charles Thatcher, 'Hurrah for Australia', reproduced in C.M.H. Clark, *Select Documents in Australian History 1851–1900,* Angus & Robertson, Sydney, 1955, pp. 105–6.

Charles E.W. Bean, *The Dreadnought of the Darling*, Alston Rivers, London, 1911, pp. 307–9.

Charles Dilke, *Greater Britain: Charles Dilke visits her new lands 1866 & 1867,* ed. Geoffrey Blainey, Methuen Haynes, North Ryde, 1985, p. 118.

Richard Twopeny, 'Young Australia', in *Town Life in Australia*, Elliot Stock, London, 1883.

Leader of the unemployed, *Argus,* 18 August 1855.

Justice H.B. Higgins quoted in Manning Clark, *Sources of Australian History*, Oxford University Press, London, 1957, p. 501.

Keith Hancock, *Australia*, Jacaranda, Brisbane, 1961, p. 55.

Henry Wrixon, *Jacob Shumate: or, the people's march, a voice from the ranks*, vol. 1, Macmillan, London, 1903, pp. 168–9.

Peter Saunders, 'What is Fair about a "Fair Go"?', *Policy,* Autumn 2004.

Carmen Lawrence, 'A Fair Go in the Classroom', <www.carmen lawrence.com>.

John Howard, address to Melbourne Press Club, 22 November 2000, <www.pm.gov.au/media/Speech/2000/speech549.cfm>.

Craig McGregor, *Profile of Australia*, Hodder & Stoughton, London, 1966, chapters 2, 15.

14. *Humour*

James Mudie, *The Felonry of New South Wales*, Lansdowne Press, Melbourne, 1964, pp. 118–19.

Charles E.W. Bean, *The Dreadnought of the Darling*, Alston Rivers, London, 1911, p. 330.

Brian Matthews in *The Oxford Companion to Australian History*, ed. Graeme Davison, John Hirst & Stuart Macintyre, Oxford University Press, Melbourne, 1998.

D.H. Lawrence, *Kangaroo*, Thomas Seltzer, New York, 1923, chapter 14.

Craig McGregor, *Profile of Australia*, Hodder & Stoughton, London, 1966, chapter 2.

15. *Newest Australians*

Andrew Riemer, *Inside Outside: life between two worlds*, ETT Imprint, Sydney, 1992, pp. 14, 14–15, 29, 30.

Morag Loh (ed.), *With Courage in their Cases: the experiences of thirty-five Italian migrant workers and their families in Australia*, Italian Federation of Emigrant Workers and their Families, Melbourne, 1980, pp. 125, 126, 127, 129–30, 131, 132.

Nguyen Xuan Thu (ed.), *Life with Past Images: personal accounts of eight Vietnamese settlers in Australia*, Phillip Institute of Technology, Coburg, 1986, p. 69.

Maria Lewitt, *No Snow in December: an autobiographical novel*, Heinemann, Melbourne, 1985, pp. 281–3.

16. *Going Native*

Russel Ward, *The Australian Legend*, Oxford University Press, Melbourne, 1958, pp. 186–7.

David Thompson, 'Origins of the Australian Football Code', BA honours thesis, La Trobe University, 2005, pp. 38–9, 48–9.

Germaine Greer, *Whitefella Jump Up: the shortest way to nationhood*, *Quarterly Essay 11*, Black Inc., Melbourne, 2003, pp. 57–8, 62.

Tim Flannery, *The Future Eaters: an ecological history of the Australasian lands and people*, Reed Books, Chatswood, 1994, pp. 391–2.

Inga Clendinnen, *Dancing with Strangers*, Text Publishing, Melbourne, 2003, p. 288.

'Mosquito' in Henry Melville's *The History of the Island of Van Diemen's Land*, Smith and Elder, London, 1835, p. 35.

Richard Broome, *Aboriginal Victorians: a history since 1800*, Allen & Unwin, Crows Nest, 2005, p. 280.

Index to Authors